THE MEANING OF ARISTOTLE'S 'ONTOLOGY'

WERNER MARX

THE MEANING OF ARISTOTLE'S 'ONTOLOGY'

THE HAGUE
MARTINUS NIJHOFF
1954

Softcover reprint of the hardcover 1st edition 1954

ISBN 978-94-011-8690-2 ISBN 978-94-011-9504-1 (eBook)
DOI 10.1007/978-94-011-9504-1

TO MY WIFE HILDE

PREFACE

This study forms part of a wider investigation which will inquire into the relationship of Ontology and Anthropology. Since the meaning of the term 'ontology' is far from clear, the immediate task is to ask the 'father of ontology' what he might have understood it to mean.

The introductory chapter emphasizes the fact that Aristotle himself never used the term 'ontology.' It should be stressed at once that, even had be used it, he could not very well have employed it to denote the discipline of ontology. For it was only during the era of the schoolmen that the vast and rich body of the *prote philosophia* came to be disciplined into classifications; these classifications reflected the Christian, – not the pagan Greek –, view of all-that-is. The *metaphysica specialis* dealing with God (theology), his creatures (psychology), and the created universe (cosmology), was differentiated from the *metaphysica generalis*, dealing with being-in-general (*ens commune*). This latter discipline amounted to the 'discipline of ontology'. [1]

We are not concerned with the meaning of the *metaphysica generalis*. We wish to approach our problem with an open mind and want to hear directly from Aristotle – on the basis of the text of the *prote philosophia* alone – which body of thought he might have called his 'ontology' and what its meaning might have been.

Yet however carefully we may attempt to 'bracket' all preconceived notions, it still remains true that it is an audacious undertaking to pose a definite question to Aristotle. More than two millenia of changing human thought cannot be eliminated, and we know very well that our question, as such, shapes and compels the answer in a definite direction which might easily be adjudged too 'modern'. Moreover, in concentrating on just one motif out of the many variegated and rich themes of the *corpus aristotelicum*, we are certain to overstress this one motif at the expense of others.

---

[1] cf. M. Heidegger, *Kant und das Problem der Metaphysik*, p. 18.

We are convinced, however, that this price must be paid. The alternative approach would be that of a self-effacing listener who is content to report, and to present, the opinions of other interpreters. This is not the way to keep ancient texts alive so that they can exert a force on present lives. The great philosophers of the past can have meaning for only us if we have the courage to engage them in a conversation, to ask questions of them and to defend the answers – as we understand them – in a determined and passionate way. Such a passion born of *philia* – love, for *sophia* – wisdom, should be easily discernible from the zeal of that merely legalistic sophistry which is anxious to be right.

It would not be a passion for *sophia* if it did not 'experience itself' as a 'finite' effort. *Philo-sophia* particularly when it attemps to interpret an ancient text – understands that at best it can only try to retrace some footsteps and to see whether they indicate one of many possible paths.

> Therefore, my Socrates ... be thou not surprised if I should not be able to give you an account which is self-consistent in all respects and is perfectly exact. You should be satisfied if my presentation is not any less – εἰκώς – similar to the truth than those given by others and you should consider that we all, I as well as you, the judges, – φύσιν ἀνθρωπίνην ἔχομεν – are of human nature only [2].

New York, July 1953 WERNER MARX

Plato, *Timaios*, 29c, 4–d, 1.

TABLE OF CONTENTS

ACKNOWLEDGMENTS

I am most grateful to Professor Karl Löwith, my teacher and friend, for encouraging me to undertake this work. Sincere thanks are due in particular to Professor Kurt Riezler for his wise counsel. Also for their interest in my work, I wish to express my appreciation to Professors Eduard Heimann, Alfred Schütz and Eugen Kullmann, colleagues in the Graduate Faculty of the New School for Social Research.*

I am indebted to Professor Hans-Georg Gadamer, of Heidelberg University, for having read the manuscript and offered valuable suggestions. My friend, the late Dr Hannes Stern (Stevens), is also gratefully remembered. Isabel C. Lundberg prepared the book for publication.

W.M.

* *Publisher's Note:* Werner Marx, Ph. D., LL. D., M. S. Sc. is a member of the Department of Philosophy in the Graduate Faculty of the New School for Social Research, New York.

INTRODUCTION

QUESTION AND METHOD

The Sciences are not under any obligation to inquire into the *meanings* of their particular endeavors. In fact, except in times of crisis, attempts at such a self-scrutiny are rightfully condemned as barren.

Philosophy, on the other hand, must eternally question itself. An interpretation of any historical system of Philosophy is suspected of dogmatic bias if it fails to raise the question at the outset: How did this particular philosophical system understand itself, wherein did this philosopher see the *meaning* of his efforts?

We raise the question: What was Aristotle's understanding of the meaning of his 'ontology'? It is particularly necessary to ask this question because Aristotle himself never called his *Metaphysics* an 'ontology'. This term was introduced only in the seventeenth century, then fell into disrepute and was rarely used by modern philosophers until it experienced a veritable renaissance in contemporary Philosophy. The various scholastic systems as well as the recent divergent ontologies, attach different meanings to the term. Etymologically, onto-logy might mean the *logos* of Being (λόγος τοῦ ὄντος) or the *logos* of beings (λογος τῶν ὄντων).

The assertion, commonly heard, that 'Aristotle is the father of ontology' does not, therefore, convey any meaning unless an answer is given to our question: What is the meaning of that particular body of thought which is now called 'Aristotle's ontology', or – what does the term 'ontology' mean in an Aristotelian context?

There is another consideration underlying our attempt to find the authentic meaning of Aristotle's 'ontology'. We shall suggest that the exposition of such meaning might serve as a reliable guide and criterion for the interpretation of many passages in the *Metaphysics*.

But how can we hope ever to be able to find the ***authentic*** meaning of Aristotle's 'ontology'?

The only way promising some degree of success is that of a systematic interpretation of relevant Aristotelian texts. However, it seems impossible to isolate specific passages in Aristotle's works and to interpret them separately. Any given concept used in a particular context presupposes knowledge of the meaning of concepts used in other parts of his works. More so than in any other philosophical system, the Aristotelian terms function as 'signs', and signs are only meaningful within a horizon of understanding that presupposes the knowledge of the entire system. Lacking knowledge of the meanings of the Aristotelian keyterms, one will misread Aristotle's signs and go in the wrong direction.

We are therefore faced with a methodological dilemma. We desire to enter immediately into the interpretation of Aristotelian texts, in order to avoid the danger of dogmatic presuppositions. But we cannot do so without having explained the meanings of decisive Aristotelian keywords.

We shall attempt to solve this dilemma by adopting the following method of procedure:

1. We shall quote that passage from Aristotle's *Metaphysics* which seems to contain the program, at least the greater parts, of the *prote philosophia* and in which he pronounces the formula which has always been considered the classical definition of the 'meaning of ontology' [1]. In quoting this passage, we shall raise questions in order to emphasize some of the keyterms which must be cleared up before an interpretation of the text can be attempted.
2. We shall next attempt clarification of these keyterms and, at the same time, follow these 'signs' to whatever additional interconnecting keywords they may lead and attempt to establish their meanings.
3. We shall then – with a full view of the interrelated and meaningful range of concepts before our eyes – attempt an interpretation of the passage quoted, in order to obtain an

[1] cf. N. Hartmann, *Zur Grundlegung der Ontologie*, p. 41 ff.

answer to our question as to what Aristotle himself might have understood his 'ontology' to mean.

4. Finally, we shall have to justify whatever answer we obtain from this interpretation, by demonstrating that this particular meaning underlies the various approaches through which Aristotle enunciated the *prote philosophia*.

CHAPTER I

THE FORMULA OF ONTOLOGY

The passages which seem to state the program, at least for the greater parts of the *prote philosophia*, are contained in the first two chapters of Book Γ of the *Metaphysics*.

The first chapter begins by very bluntly pronouncing, in rather cryptic language, the formula which is still celebrated today as the ideal formula of any ontology [1]:

> There is an *episteme* (ἐπιστήμη) that contemplates (θεωρεῖ) being as being (ὂν ᾗ ὄν) and that which belongs to it per se.

What is the meaning of *episteme* in Aristotle's system; in particular, what is its meaning when it is an *episteme* that 'contemplates'? What does 'being' mean for Aristotle and what does the formula 'being as being' signify? In short, is it a particular kind of *episteme* that directs its contemplation to 'being as being'?

The following sentences of the chapter do not throw any light on these questions but raise new ones.

> It is not the same as any of those that are called particular inquiries; for none of these treats universally (καθόλου) of being as being. They cut off a part of it and contemplate what happens (τὸ συμβεβηκός) to belong to such a part as for instance the mathematical science does.

We learn from these sentences that, in contradistinction to 'other sciences', the *episteme*, defined in the preceding sentences, treats of 'being' not in a piecemeal fashion but 'as a whole' and

---

[1] cf. N. Hartmann, *op. cit.*, p. 41: 'Aristoteles hatte daher ganz Recht, die *Prote Philosophia* als Wissenschaft vom ὂν ᾗ ὂν zu bezeichnen' . . . p. 42: 'Man darf sich diese Formel ohne weiteres zu eigen machen. Sie ist zwar sehr formal, aber in ihrer Art unuebertrefflich'.

treats of it 'universally'. But what do 'being-as-a-whole', and a 'universal' *episteme* of being, imply?

The next sentences emphasize the goal of this *episteme*. It turns out to be the same goal as that of all 'wisdom' (σοφία). The preceding three books repeatedly define the aim of wisdom [2]. It is *episteme* of the first causes (τὰ πρῶτα αἴτια) and of the principles (ἀρχαί). It is primary philosophy (πρώτη φιλοσοφία) in this sense [3]. The 'primary' aim of philosophy is now established more precisely:

> Now since we are searching for the principles and ultimate causes, clearly there must be some nature (φύσις) to which these principles and causes belong necessarily and per se [4].

So this *episteme* which is described as a 'searching' for the principles and ultimate causes aims at a knowledge about a 'nature'. At the same time we learn something about that nature: it is a nature to which principles and causes 'belong necessarily and per se'. What sort of nature is this? What kind of searching is it that seeks to find such a nature?

The closing sentences of the first chapter contain a very strange argument:

> If then those who searched for the elements of beings (τῶν ὄντων) [5] were seeking the same principles, then the elements must have been elements of being (τοῦ ὄντος) [6] not by accident but *qua* being (ἀλλ ᾗ ὄν) [7]. Therefore, it is of being as being that we must grasp the first causes [8].

The argument seems to run as follows: I (Aristotle) know that my predecessors looked for the elements of the things-that-are, by which is meant, of 'be-ings'. These necessary elements of beings belong, however, to the nature of being; they are its 'first causes'. Therefore, it follows that we (the students of the Lyceum) should follow our great predecessors by looking for the first causes of 'being as being'.

---

[2] cf. *Meta.*, 981b, 29–982a, 1–3.
[3] cf. *Ibid.*, 993a, 15.
[4] We translate φύσεώς τινος as the Possessive Genetive of φύσις τις.
[5] Note the Genetive Plural.
[6] Note the Genetive Singular.
[7] Note the Singular.
[8] διὸ καὶ ἡμῖν τοῦ ὄντος ᾗ ὂν τὰς πρώτας αἰτίας ληπτέον.

So, rather than answering the questions contained in the preceding sentences, this sentence, meant probably as an exhortation to his students, glosses over whatever differences there might be between Aristotle's philosophy and that of his predecessors.

The opening paragraphs of the second chapter give rise to further questions and bring up additional keyterms which must be introduced before an interpretation of the entire section can be attempted. This passage is of decisive importance for our thesis. Our translation is close to the one presented by Ross [9], but differs from his in some respects:

> One speaks about 'being' (*on*) in many ways, but all-that-is is related (*pros hen*) to a unity and one certain nature (*physis*) and is not *homonym*, but is related in the same way as everything that is healthy is related to health either in the way that it preserves health or in the way that it produces health or in the way that is a symptom of health or because it is capable of it. And that which is medical is related to medical art: either it is called medical because it possesses it or because it is naturally adapted to it or because it is a function of medical art. And we find other expressions of speech used similar to these examples. So there are many ways in which one speaks about being but all are related to one principle. One speaks of some as beings because they are *ousiai* [substances] others because they are affections of *ousia*, others because they are a process towards *ousia*, or destructions or privations or qualities of *ousia*, or productive or generative of *ousia*, or of things which are relative to *ousia* or negations of one of these or of substance itself. It is for this reason that one even says of not-being that it 'is' not-being.

Aristotle thus refers his listeners to the ways *one speaks about* being. What is the meaning and function of speaking? Speaking, he says, reveals that all-that-is is related to one 'nature'. Is this the same kind of nature to which he referred in the preceding chapter? Now he gives to nature the name: *ousia*, substance. What does *ousia* mean? We note that he also speaks of *ousiai*, substances; is *ousiai* just the plural of *ousia*, or does the context of these passages reveal a clue to the difference between this singular *ousia* and plural *ousiai* which is at variance with usual and everyday ways of understanding.

[9] W. D. Ross, *Metaphysics*, Vol. VIII, A–D Book I, Ch. 2.

This question leads us to a decisive preliminary problem: Were all these keyterms meant by Aristotle as 'signs' for men in their ***natural*** – everyday – attitude, or were they meant as 'signs' for the students of the Lyceum, the philo-sophers who are in a *philo-sophical* attitude?

We have, first, to try to answer this basic question; only then can we hope to be able to clarify the meaning of these signs or keyterms in an adequate way.

CHAPTER II

THE KEYTERMS

1. The philo-sophical attitude [1]

The last sentence of the first chapter [2] as well as the last sentence of the first paragraph of the second chapter [3] show in unequivocal language that Aristotle spoke here as a philosopher to philosophers, and that he spoke in a 'philosophical attitude' about a 'philosophical subject-matter'. He therefore did not speak in what, following modern parlance, we shall call a 'natural attitude' [4] about a 'natural subject-matter'. Aristotle was very careful to set the life and activities of the philosopher [5] apart from the life and activities of other men [6], although he emphasized that every man could become a lover of wisdom – a *philosophos* [7]. Yet, while 'all men strive to see and know' [8], such striving does not by itself bring about the actuality (ἐνέργεια) of the 'theoretical life' [9]. The actuality of the theoretical life is clearly differentiated both from that of the life of mere *empeiria* [10] and

---

[1] ἕξις

[2] *Meta.*, Book Γ, 1003a, 30: therefore, it is of being as being that 'we too' must grasp the first causes.

[3] *Ibid.*, 1103b, 19: if, then, substance is the primary thing, it is of substance that 'the philosopher' must grasp the principles and causes.

[4] e.g. as used by E. Husserl in *Ideen zu einer reinen Phaenomenologie und Phaenomenologischen Philosophie*, Bd. 1, S. 57. We do not want to use the designation 'empirical' because Aristotle attaches a particular meaning to *empeiria*. Nor do we want to create the impression that we denied that Aristotle's method is an empirical one in the sense that he always starts from the concrete beings as they present themselves. P. 25ff.

[5] *Nicomachean Ethics*, 1177a, 14.

[6] cf. *Meta.*, 982a, 5 ff; 982a, 20 ff; 982b, 27 ff; 1072b, 18 ff; 1074b, 15 ff. *Nic. Eth.*, 1097b, 23 ff; 1141a, 9 ff.

[7] cf. *Ibid.*; also *De Anima*, Book III, Ch. 4.

[8] *Meta.*, 980, 22. πάντες ἄνθρωποι τοῦ εἰδέαι ὀρέγονται.
The translation must bring out the 'seeing' implied in the word εἰδέναι.

[9] cf. *Ibid.*, the description 981b, 26 ff and 982a, 16 ff and *Nic. Eth.*, 1177a, 12 ff.

[10] cf. *Meta.*, 980b, 26 ff.

from that of *techne* and *episteme*[11]. The man of *techne* and *episteme* is already a great deal advanced over the man of mere *empeiria*. He already 'sees the differences' (διαφοράς) by virtue of *logos* (λόγος) and (εἶδος); he directs his attention to 'universals' (καθόλου) rather than to singulars[12], and knows the 'causes' (αἰτίαι). However, the actuality of his life is still fundamentally different from that of the man who 'loves wisdom' (φιλό-σοφος)[13].

The lover of wisdom strives to 'see the differences'[14]; but they are of a different kind[15] and his attitude (ἕξις) is different from that of other men. For he is a man who is open enough to be amazed (θαυμάζειν)[16]. Amazement can overcome him, it 'acts on him' so that he must 'suffer' the 'passion of his love'[17]. Realizing that he does not know anything[18] and that therefore everything is questionable, he is gripped by a passion-for-wisdom and strives to overcome his 'agnostic' state so that in the light of wisdom[19] he might grasp more and more (μᾶλλον) until he can 'see' the ultimate causes and principles[20]. He does not have any other purpose. For this is the good (τἀγαθόν)[21] for him, the human good (τὸ ἀνθρώπινον ἀγαθόν).

We must, moreover, try to show that Aristotle not only set the life of the philosopher apart from the life of other men but also set the 'philosophical' apart from the 'natural' attitude, and separated the subject-matter of philosophy from the subject-matter of 'natural' thought. This task leads us directly into the discussion of the relevant keyterms.

Such a discussion might, however, easily be criticized as being too 'modern'. Admittedly today's interpretations cannot help being influenced by modern Philosophy. The subject matter of German Idealistic Philosophy from Kant to Hegel had just this goal of setting the autonomous movement of philosophical thinking apart from merely 'natural' thinking and then describ-

---

11 More correct: *Ibid.*, 980b, 26: *techne* and *logismos*.
12 cf. *Ibid.*, 980b, 29 ff.
13 *Ibid.*, 981b, 26 ff, 982a, 16 ff.
14 *Meta.*, 980a, 23.
15 cf. *Ibid.*, 981b, 29 ff and *De An.*, 429b, 21 ff.
16 cf. *Ibid.*, 982b, 11 ff.
17 cf. *Ibid.*, 982b, 19. See also, p. 64 *infra*.
18 *Ibid.*, 982b, 17 ff.
19 *De An.*, 430a, 14.
20 *Meta.*, 981b, 29.
21 cf. *Nic. Eth.*, 1094a, 1 ff.

ing the structure and development of philosophical thought.

But Kant did not discover this philosophical faculty in man. He discovered it only in the sense of *un*covering it: he made visible that which was there already but was not clearly realized before. It is our contention that Aristotle was, to a great extent, already clearly aware of the different character of the 'philosophical' over against the 'natural' attitude and of their different subject-matters.

2. *Episteme*

Aristotle, in the First Chapter of Book Γ of the *Metaphysics*, called the knowledge of 'being as being' an ἐπιστήμη and called the activity of *episteme* a θεωρεῖν. At the end of the following chapter this activity is expressly stated to be that of a 'philosopher'. We now reformulate our first question: What does the '*episteme* that contemplates being' mean as an activity of a philosopher?

The *Nicomachean Ethics* defines '*episteme* as such' [22], on the one hand, and on the other, '*episteme* in connection with wisdom'.

It is important for us to note that the subject matter of either kind of *episteme* is something that 'exists necessarily' [23] and is 'eternal' [24], meaning 'that which neither comes into existence nor perishes' (ἀγένητα καὶ ἄφθαρτα) [25]. Yet, the activity of *episteme* as such is to 'deduct' or demonstrate (ἀπόδειξις) [26] from these 'necessary and eternal' principles. It is an *apodeiktic* activity [27]. But while this activity deals with these universal and necessary principles, it cannot, as such, reach them.

> The first principles from which *apodeiktic episteme* is derived cannot themselves be reached by *episteme* as such [28].

Is it possible for man to 'reach' these necessary and eternal principles? Aristotle answers: 'It is possible'. But this affirmative

---

22 *Nic. Eth.*, 1139b, 18, 1141a, 3.
23 *Ibid.*, 1139b, 24.
24 *Ibid.*, 1139b, 24–25.
25 *Ibid.*, 1139b, 25.
26 *Ibid.*, 1141a, 1–3.
27 *Ibid.*, 1141a, 3.
28 *Ibid.*, 1140b, 33.

answer must be understood with a paalification [29] which denotes the philosopher's situation 'in-between' [30] the possession-of-power and lack-of-power. It is this attitude of in-between that radically differentiates his position from the certainty of attitude of the *apodeiktic episteme* as such.

Surely, a philosopher will also 'deduct' apodeiktically. But if this is all he strives to do, he will never reach the first principles. This kind of *episteme* is not sufficient. It must become 'wisdom'. It must be 'inspired' in an entirely different way. Νοῦς must join *episteme* as such and thereby determine the philosopher in his search for 'the ultimate causes and principles'.

> It is Νοῦς that apprehends the principles [31].

> Only because 'Νοῦς has joined *episteme*' [32],

> can the wise man not only know the conclusions following from these principles but also have the truth of these principles themselves [33].

Only because *sophia* is Νοῦς and *episteme* as such will the philosopher be able

> to attain a knowledge which is a possession of the head [34].

The head, in this sense, means the highest 'organizing principle', the knowledge of which is a possession of knowledge as knowledge [35].

It is therefore Νοῦς which determines the character of philosophical thinking. We have to inquire into the meaning of Νοῦς, to be able to understand the significance of the *episteme* which is in the service of the *sophia* of the *philo-sophos*.

3. *Noesis and Noeton*

As the sacred word Νοῦς is sounded, the entire tradition of Greek thought comes to life. Realizing that the greatest mystery

---

[29] *Ibid.*, 1141a, 9 ff.
[30] cf. Plato, *Parmenides*, 130E ff.: μεταξύ.
[31] *Nic. Eth.*, 1141a, 9. λείπεται νοῦν εἶναι τῶν ἀρχῶν.
[32] *Ibid.*, 1141a, 19. ἡ σοφία νοῦς καὶ ἐπιστήμη.
[33] *Ibid.*, 1141a, 17–20. ἀληθεύειν περὶ τὰς ἀρχάς.
[34] *Ibid.*, 1141a, 19. κεφαλὴν ἔχουσα ἐπιστήμη τῶν τιμιωτάτων.
[35] cf. also *Meta.*, 1072b, 23.

lies in the self-transparency, in the intelligibility of all-that-is, Presocratic Philosophy gave the name Νοῦς both to the cause of intelligibility and to the state-of-intelligibility. Several thinkers held that Νοῦς is even prior to *kosmos*, the order of all-that-is; and it was in this sense, that Anaxagoras exclaimed: Νοῦς reigns over all [36].

It was Parmenides who gave man a particular role under the reign and in the realm of Νοῦς. That which Νοῦς thinks: the *noema* (νόημα), the activity of thinking *noein* (νοεῖν), and *noesis* (νόησις), designating a human activity, are pronounced to be the same [37] in the sense that thought must be 'thought by man' [38]. He surely designated it as the role and task of man to assist in the unveiling of the order, to bring about the self-transparency of the *kosmos*.

Aristotle deals in *De Anima* [39] with the way in which Νοῦς acts 'in or on' [40] the soul of man. The act of *noesis* – as the particular activity of the philosopher – as well as its subject-matter, the *noeton*, is described in the *Nicomachean Ethics* [41] and in the Seventh Chapter of the Twelfth Book of the *Metaphysics*, the Theology [42]. Aristotle shows in the *Nicomachean Ethics* how [43] the activity which is determined by Νοῦς – when carried out in the best possible way (κατ' ἀρετήν) – constitutes man's highest possibility-to-be; in fact, it is so high that it is 'not human any more' [44] 'but divine' (θεῖον) [45].

The *Nicomachean Ethics* leaves the question undecided, whether Aristotle actually means that the activity (νόησις) and the subject-matter (νοητόν) of Philosophy are identical with or are only similar to those of ὁ θεὸς (divinity). Some passages in the *Metaphysics* could be read as if there existed a difference only

---

[36] cf. H. Diels, *Die Fragmente der Vorsokratiker*, Bd. I. Frag. 12 : 18. Περὶ Φύσεως: πάντων νοῦς κρατεῖ.

[37] *Ibid.*, Frag. 8 : 34, Περὶ Φύσεως: ταὐτὸν δ'ἐστὶ νοεῖν τε καὶ οὕνεκεν ἔστι νόημα.

[38] cf. also H. G. Gadamer, *Zur Vorgeschichte d. Metaphysik*, p. 72.

[39] *De An.*, Book III, Ch. 4–8.

[40] We need not discuss within the context of this paper whether Νοῦς is a 'transcendental or an immanent power'. cf. *De An.*, 430a, 18 ff together with *Nic. Eth.*, 1178a, 1 and 1178a, 8.

[41] cf. *Nic. Eth.*, particularly 1178a, 12 ff.

[42] *Meta.*, 1072b, 15 ff.

[43] *Nic. Eth.*, 1177a, 11 ff.

[44] *Ibid.*, 1177a, 28.

[45] *Ibid.*, 1177a, 27 ff.

to the extent that 'man enjoys this state for a short time' [46]. But these passages should be read together with Aristotle's exposition of Νοῦς in *De Anima* where it is made clear that the human *noesis* remains dependent on the *phantasmata* [47], while the divine thinking, beginning absolutely on its own, is unqualifiedly 'spontaneous' [48]. Accordingly, in our view, the human *noesis* as well as the subject-matter of *theoria* can never be 'the same' but are only 'similar' to those of ὁ θεὸς. It is sufficient for our particular purposes to point again to the fact that Aristotle indubitably meant to set the philosophical activity and the subject-matter of philosophy strictly apart from all other human activities by comparing them to the divine activity and the divine *theoria*.

We now have to analyze the relevant passages to explain the philosophical activity, *noesis*, and its subject matter, the *noeton*. It is our contention that Aristotle stood firmly on traditional grounds. In *De Anima* [49] he quotes Anaxagoras and his view about the power of Νοῦς:

> Νοῦς, in order as Anaxagoras says, to dominate...

Νοῦς therefore is for Aristotle also 'the ruler' and he, too, holds that Νοῦς exerts its power by making the *kosmos* self-transparent. The Νοῦς ποιητικός 'by virtue of which all things become' [50] is likened to

> a positive state of light... [51]

and the activity of light is an

> actuality which is transparent [52].

Man fulfills his role of assisting in the unveiling of the *kosmos* only if and when he actually thinks, *i.e.*, intuitively apprehends. Therefore Aristotle asserts in *De Anima* that the human mind, from the point of view of man, is a *dynamis* only and has no nature of its own [53].

---

[46] *Meta.*, 1072b, 11 and 1072b, 15–1072b, 23.
[47] *De An.*, 431a, 14; 431b, 2; 432a, 9 ff.
[48] cf. *Meta.*, 1072b, 15 ff.
[49] *De An.*, 429a, 19.
[50] *Ibid.*, 430a, 15.
[51] *Loc. cit.*
[52] *Op. cit.*, 418b, 9.
[53] *Ibid.*, 429a, 24 ff, but cf. 430a, 20 and 431a, 2.

> It is not a real thing before it actually thinks [54].

> ...potentially (δύναμις) whatever is thinkable though actually (ἐνέργεια) it is nothing until it has thought [55].

The act of thinking, *noesis*, in turn obtains its nature from its object, the *noeton*, about which it thinks. While Aristotle clearly recognizes that *noesis*, on the one hand, and the *noeton* or *noumenon*, the object of thought, on the other are as such different:

> to be in the act of thinking (*noesis*) and to be an object of thought are not the same... [56]

he emphasizes that

> in some cases, the knowledge (*episteme*) is its subject-matter (*pragma*). [57]

The cases he specifies as follows:

> In the productive Sciences, it is *ousia* or the *to ti en einai* of the object, matter omitted, and in the theoretical sciences, the *logos* or the *noesis* is the subject-matter (*pragma*) [58].

In all these cases: 'The *noesis* and *noumenon* are one' [59].

The same thought is expressed in various passages in *De Anima*, where Aristotle with special reference to the *episteme theoretike* states:

> In the case of objects which involve no matter, what thinks and what is thought are identical. For *episteme theoretike* and its *noeton* are identical [60].

In the *Metaphysics* Aristotle then describes the way the *noesis* and *noeton* become identical:

> And Νοῦς thinks on itself to the extent that it participates in the object of thought (*noeton*). It becomes the *noeton* when it touches and intuitively apprehends its objects so that *noesis* and the *noeton* are the same [61].

---

54 *Loc. cit.*
55 *Op. cit.*, 429b, 23.
56 *Meta.*, 1074b, 37.
57 *Ibid.*, 1075a, 1.
58 *Ibid.*, 1075a, 2 ff.
59 *Ibid.*, 1075a, 4.
60 *De An.*, 430a, 4.
61 *Meta.*, 1072*b*, 22.

Such participation is characterized as an active possession of the thought as thought.

> For that which is capable of receiving the *noeton* and the *ousia* is Νοῦς. But it is active when it possesses it [62].

It is this active possession of thought as thought which is called *theoria* [63].

While the subject-matter of divine *noesis*, divine *theoria*, can, for reasons set forth, [64] only be the act of thinking, the *noesis* itself, and therefore *noesis noeseos* [65], human *noesis*, unlike the divine, can have various subject-matters. It can be Νοῦς or *noesis* itself [66] or the principles and ultimate causes [67] (among them ὁ θεός) [68], or the *to ti en einai* or *ousia* [69]. We shall discuss later the extent to which these various subject-matters of human *theoria* ultimately coalesce [70]. For our present purposes it is important to emphasize again that in order to be the subject-matter of philosophical *noesis*, they must be *noeta* – and that means 'possessed in thought by thought' [71].

Further we learn in the same chapter [72] that these *noeta* have the character of *adiaireta* or *asyntheta i.e.*, they are 'indivisibles', a keyterm which we shall have to explain. They are contrasted with *syntheta*. The human mind, in everyday empirical thinking, is concerned with 'synthetic things' only, while philosophical *noesis*, in the few moments man can enjoy it [73], grasps (θιγεῖν), touches the *asyntheta*.

De Anima, as well as the Tenth Chapter of the Ninth Book of the *Metaphysics*, deals with the way human thinking grasps the *asyntheta*, but here this problem is taken up in conjunction with another important keyterm *aletheia*, truth. We follow the signs by which the Aristotelian keyterms function in order to learn

---

62 *Ibid.*, 1072b, 22.
63 *Ibid.*, 1072b, 24.
64 cf. *Ibid.*, 1074b, 15 ff.
65 *Ibid.*, 1074b, 35.
66 cf. *De An.*, 430a, 2 and *Meta.*, 1075a, 3.
67 cf. *Meta.*, 981b, 28 ff and 982b, 1 ff.
68 cf. *Ibid.*, 983a, 5 ff.
69 *Ibid.*, 1075a, 2 and *De An.*, 430b, 26.
70 cf. also *infra*, p. 61 for the later discussion.
71 *Meta.*, 1072b, 22.
72 *Ibid.*, 1075a, 5 ff.
73 *Ibid.*, 1072b, 14 ff, 1072b, 24.

more about the character of philosophical *noesis* and of its subject-matter, the *noeton*.

4. *Aletheuein and Aletheia*

Aristotle gives a new name to the philosophical *noesis* when he deals in the Ninth Book of the *Metaphysics* with the way man touches (θιγεῖν) [74] the *asyntheta* [75]. Here the noetic activity is characterized as an *aletheuein*, an attaining to *aletheia*, truth.

There are two basic meanings of *aletheuein* and *aletheia* alive in the *corpus aristotelicum*. One of them comes close to what we today associate with the meaning of Truth. In *De Interpretatione* Aristotle implies that Truth is

> bringing the experiences of the soul into correspondence with the things [76].

It was this concept of Truth that gained entrance into the *Book of Definitions* by Isaac Israeli and was from there taken over by Thomas of Aquinas [77]. For him Truth is always an *adaequatio intellectus et rei* or a *correspondentia*, or a *convenientia* between the thought (as expressed in a judgment) and the thing [78]. The same meaning underlies all modern epistemology [79].

There is, however, an older meaning of *aletheia* alive in Aristotle's works. In Presocratic tradition [80], *a-letheia* seems to have implied a state of manifestedness in which *Lethe* has been overcome, a state of un-concealedness; and *aletheuein* correspondingly meant: to un-conceal, to take out of the state of *Lethe*. The un-concealing effort on the part of man presupposes in a sense the state of unconcealedness within which this activity can act: it presupposes that there is something that can be gathered as *aletheia* [81].

---

[74] *Ibid.*, 1051b, 24.
[75] *Ibid.*, 1051b, 18.
[76] *De Int.*, 16A, 5.
[77] *Summa Theologica* Qu. 16, Art. 12, Obj. 2, which refers to Isaac Israeli.
[78] But the truth of the thing, in turn, was guaranteed through its own *correspondentia* with the 'idea', as conceived by God.
[79] cf. I. Kant, *Kritik der Reinen Vernunft*, pp. 82, 83, 100, 350.
[80] cf. K. Riezler, *Parmenides*, p. 15, on the subject of *aletheia* and the Presocratics particularly.
[81] cf. M. Heidegger, *Sein und Zeit*, p. 226 ff., on the sense in which 'Wahrheit ist vorausgesetzt'.

As Plato later formulated it in the *Meno:*

> How will you search for that which you do not know and how can you plan to search for that which you do not know and if you found it how could you recognize that which you do not know? [82]

The assumption of the traditional version of Truth seems therefore to have been the following: All-that-is is in a way manifest or visible and it is up to man to gather it in its truth and make in fully manifest. Aristotle, in *De Anima* and in the *Metaphysics*, taught that such gathering-in occurs in two ways, depending on whether things are *syntheta* or *asyntheta*. If they are *syntheta*, then man 'gathers-in their truth' through discursive thinking, *dianoeistai*. In empirical, everyday kind of reasoning man in a 'judging way' attaches predicates to a subject. This unity [83] brought about by the unifying force of the Νοῦς Ποιητικός [84] can be in truth or in error, depending on whether such combining is done in accordance with the way things 'are in their truth' [85]. The important point here is that even in this case of discursive thinking about synthetic things Aristotle clearly bases himself on the traditional meaning of Truth:

> It is not because we think truly that you are pale that you *are* pale but because you are pale we who say this have the truth [86].

Thus, to say, λέγειν, is a collecting, a combining of something pregiven. This is, indeed, the traditional meaning of *legein*: to bring pregiven elements into a 'unity' so that their sense or meaning comes to light. This is the reason why *legein* can mean 'to understand' as well as to explain and to say; its unifying role underlies all three meanings [87].

The second way of gathering-in-the-truth occurs through the act of *noesis* which, as we have already seen, directs itself towards something 'indivisible', an *adiaireton* or *asyntheton*.

---

[82] Plato, *Meno*, 80d, 8.

[83] cf. *De An.*, 430b, 4; *Meta.*, 1051b, 34. (ἓν μέν ἐστιν).

[84] *De An.*, 430b, 4: 'in each and every case that which unifies is 'Νοῦς'. cf. also 430a, 14 ff.

[85] cf. *Meta.*, 1051b, 3 ff; also *De An.*, 430a, 26 ff.

[86] *Meta.*, 1051b, 7.

[87] cf. M. Heidegger *Logos Festschrift fuer H. Jantzen*, regarding the original meaning of λέγειν.

Here Νοῦς Ποιητικός unites [88] by creating a different unity (τὸ δὲ ἕν) [89]. Here, understanding is not a combining of pregiven predicates with a *subjectum* but is one act of grasping something pregiven as an *asyntheton*. Man can either grasp it or not succeed in grasping it. Here error in the above sense is not possible: when the philosopher fails to 'see', then he is 'blind'. [90].

We must now try to reach a better understanding of the way in which this unity of an *asyntheton* constitutes itself in such an 'unconcealing activity'. The *asyntheton* which the Twelfth Book of the *Metaphysics* designates as the subject-matter of philosophical *noesis* is in *De Anima* described as a simple unit (ἁπλᾶ) [91]. Aristotle here contrasts the *asyntheta* with the *syntheta* and we are therefore permitted to deduce that *a-syntheta*, not being synthesized, are unities in themselves: they are wholes. Aristotle mentions in the same chapter [92] three kinds of *asyntheta*: the first, qualitatively (though not quantitatively) indivisibles like a line; the second, quantitatively indivisibles like a point; and a third, the important one for us, 'that which is something indivisible in what Νοῦς thinks'.

This passage should be read together with other parts of Chapters 6 and 7 of *De Anima*, as well as with the corresponding parts of the *Metaphysics* to which reference was made earlier.

The *noesis* un-conceals, gathers-in, in their truth, the *noemata* or, as *Aristotle* calls them subsequently, the *prota noemata*, [93] which man by virtue of a different power or the same power in a different state [94] apprehends 'in' [95] the *phantasmata*. These *prota noemata* are *einai* [96] or *to ti en einai* [97] or *ousia* [98]; all these fundamental notions will be explained at a later point. Aristotle gives as an example: in philosophical *noesis* man grasps, gathers in, un-conceals, *e.g.*, the fleshness of the flesh.

---

88 *De An.*, 430b, 5.
89 *Meta.*, 1051b, 35.
90 cf. *Ibid.*, 1051b, 32; 1052a, 3ff; *De An.*, 430b, 27 ff.
91 *De An.*, 430a, 26.
92 *Ibid.*, 430b, 6–20.
93 *Ibid.*, 432a, 10.
94 *Ibid.*, 429b, 21.
95 *Ibid.*, 432a, 14; also 431a, 14; 431b, 13.
96 *Ibid.*, 429b, 15; *Meta.*, 1051b, 29; 1051b, 33.
97 *De An.*, 429b, 18 and 430b, 29; also *Meta.*, 1075a, 3.
98 *Meta.*, 1075a, 3; 1051b, 27.

> The *einai* of flesh is apprehended by something different either wholly separate from the sensitive faculty or related to it as a bent line to the same line when it has straightened out [99].

In the Ninth Book of the *Metaphysics* this *aletheuein* is described in an entirely parallel way as a gathering-in, a touching of the unity [100] of an asynthetic whole [101]. Here that which is 'touched' is throughout called *einai* (and not *to ti en einai* or *ousia* [102]). The *einai* is the *asyntheton*, the indivisible, the whole.

The problem is to explain how this whole makes itself manifest *i.e.*, constitutes itself in its unity [103] in and through the unconcealing act (*aletheuein*), the 'gathering-in' of its truth (*aletheia*).

This 'process of the *aletheuein* of an *asyntheton* in its *aletheia*' occurs through philosophical *noesis*. In Chapter 10 of the Ninth Book of the *Metaphysics*, which deals exclusively with this problem, Aristotle emphasizes, in fact, that the 'seeing' of the *asyntheta* is a *noein* [104]. The *asyntheta* either make themselves manifest in constituting a unity in and through the human *noesis* and thus arrive in their *aletheia* [105], or they remain in *Lethe*.

Truth of *asyntheta* therefore occurs in the noetic act. We find in *De Anima* an indication of how Aristotle visualized this process. Here he deals with the way the *eide* make themselves manifest in and through human thinking. They are potentially already 'on their seat' [106]; they are pregiven 'in a sense' [107]. However, they get actually to their seat only in and through the act of human thinking. For only then can they fulfill their true nature and function: to grant sight, to make things seeable in their whatness. We also learn here that this work is accomplished by the Νοῦς Ποιητικός which is compared to the human hand that, as an organ of organs, 'makes tools to function as tools' [108].

The *eidos eidoos* as the Νοῦς Ποιητικός makes the *eide* [109]

---

99 *De An.*, 429b, 15 ff.
100 *Meta.*, 1051b, 35.
101 *Ibid.*, 1051b, 18 ff.
102 *Loc. cit.*
103 cf. *De An.*, 430a, 14, together with 430b, 5 and *Meta.*, 1051b, 35.
104 *Meta.*, 1051b, 32 and 1052a, 1.
105 *Ibid.*, 1052a, 1.
106 *De An.*, 429a, 28; however, as such, they are 'actual'. cf. *Meta.*, 1051b, 27.
107 cf. *De An.*, 417b, 22; the *episteme* of the καθόλου are 'in a sense within the soul'.
108 *Ibid.*, 432a, 2 ff.
109 *Ibid.*, 430a, 15.

manifest; such a 'making' occurs through an act of unification [110] which is different for *syntheta* and *asyntheta*. The act of unification is discussed in terms of 'truth and error' and in the case of *asyntheta* Aristotle expressly explains that truth is attained through *noesis*. Here in *De Anima*, absolutely parallel with the treatment in the Ninth Book of the *Metaphysics*, Aristotle explains that such a *noesis* can either 'see' or be blind. Only if and when man 'sees' does the unity of the truth of a whole constitute itself.

We therefore arrive at the realization that Aristotle conceived of the truth of a-synthetic wholes as pregiven in the same sense; they, as such, are therefore always actual [111]. But they make themselves manifest only if and when they constitute themselves as unities [112]. This occurs in and through the act of philosophical *Noesis*. The *Noesis* is therefore characterized as an act of unconcealing of *aletheuein* of pregiven wholes. We further learn, again only through several cryptic remarks, that human *noesis* in and through which the manifestation of pregiven *asyntheta* occurs, acts 'beyond chronological time'. In *De Anima* [113], explaining the meaning of *asyntheta*, Aristotle states, for example, that the *asyntheton*, length, is grasped in 'undivided time', although, as he points out, time is divided in the same manner as the line. He thus refers to the division into time dimensions of past, present and future. He repeats the same thought again when he mentions those *asyntheta* which 'Νοῦς thinks in their *noemata*' [114]. In the *Metaphysics* he gives the example of grasping the circleness of a circle and states that the circleness of a circle remains always the 'same' [115].

The properties of a circle, inhering in its circleness, manifest themselves, *i.e.*, constitute themselves as a unity in the act of human *noesis*, as the same pregiven momenta of a pregiven unity. They present themselves beyond the time dimensions of future, past and present.

---

[110] *Ibid.*, 430b, 5.
[111] *Meta.*, 1051b, 27.
[112] *Ibid.*, 1051b, 35.
[113] *De An.*, 430b, 6 ff.
[114] *Ibid.*, 430, 16.
[115] cf. *Meta.*, 1052a, 5 ff.

We might now briefly recapitulate the results of our investigation up to this point:

1. Philosophical *noesis* is treated by Aristotle as an attitude *kat exochen*; it occurs as an attitude different from the 'natural' human attitude.
2. It is a 'possessing' of subject-matters of thought, *noeta*, in the realization that they are thought by thought or grasped through intuition. It is an unconcealing of these *noeta* which occurs beyond chronological time.
3. The *noeta*, the subject-matter of philosophical *noesis*, are pregiven wholes. Forced by the power of the Νοῦς Ποιητικός they make themselves manifest by constituting themselves in and through the noetic act as unities of momenta.
4. These noetic wholes were designated by Aristotle either as *einai* or as *to ti en einai* or as *ousia*.

In the same chapter of the Ninth Book of the *Metaphysics*, in which Aristotle deals with the *aletheia*, he characterizes the 'noetic whole' as 'being', using the Greek *einai* or *on*. It is here that he briefly describes *on* as that which is 'neither coming nor ceasing to be' [116], and thereby characterizes the subject-matter of philosophical *noesis* as being 'beyond time'.

We shall now turn to the interpretation of the passages in Book Γ, quoted above, because they contain the 'formula of Aristotle's ontology'.

[116] *Ibid.*, 1051b, 29.

CHAPTER III

THE *PHYSIS EINAI* OR *ON*

It will be recalled that Book Γ opens with the statement:

> There is an *episteme* that contemplates being as being...

and that this *episteme* was characterized by Aristotle as a

> searching for the principles and ultimate causes...

and that he asserted:

> ...there must be a *physis* to which these principles and causes belong necessarily and per se [1].

We know now that the 'episteme that contemplates being as being' has the character of a philosophical *noesis*, of an unconcealing act; and that its subject-matter is a *noeton* which Aristotle described as an asynthetic whole that is pregiven and manifests itself, *i.e.* constitutes itself in the noetic act as the unity of its momenta.

We stated at the outset that Aristotle opens the Book Γ in an abrupt way. We remarked that he presents the 'formula of ontology' to his readers in a rather cryptic language. Now, we realize, there was no need for him to explain at length why, and in which sense, this *episteme* is 'a contemplating about being as being' because his students must have known all along that he was treating of a subject-matter in a noetic way and that he therefore might have been concerned with 'being' as the one subject-matter (*noeton*) of the philosophical *noesis* [2].

The 'formula' is only a restatement of a basic proposition which could not have been anything new to the students of the Lyceum. Aristotle offers in this chapter only one further expla-

---

[1] *Ibid.*, 1003a, 21, 29, 28.

[2] Regarding the other subject-matters of philosophical *noesis* cf. p. 15 *supra*.

nation of the *noeton*, being, while devoting most of the following considerations to an explanation of the *noeton*, substance.

The additional clarification of 'being' consists in its characterization as a *Physis*.

The various definitions of the terms *physis* in Book Δ of the *Metaphysics* [3] as well as those in the *Physics* [4] do not seem to express the full meaning of the word as Aristotle used it in the above context. Yet the full breadth of the traditional meaning of the word *physis* was still alive in Aristotle's thinking despite the criticism he directed against his predecessors [5].

Whatever the divergent interpretations of the word *physis* in Presocatic philosophy might have been, they are, according to Aristotle himself [6], the 'same' or 'analogous' insofar as φύσις denotes an ἀρχή [7].

Physis meant the principle by virtue of which particular 'natures' are natures. *Physis* in this sense is the 'natureness' of particular natures. This natureness was conceived as the unity of a whole of momenta, borne together [8], causing all the *metabolai* but remaining the same 'beyond time' [9].

Summing up his various definitions in Book Δ of the *Metaphysics*, Aristotle, in line with that traditional concept, seems to differentiate between a *physis qua* natureness and the factual *physeis*. For here he states:

> From what has been said it is plain that *physis* in the primary sense (*prote physis*) is the *ousia* of those (*physeis*) which have an *arche* of *kinesis* in themselves [10].

And in the last sentences of the Seventh Book of the *Metaphysics* [11] he calls *physis* that which constitutes the particular

---

3 *Meta.*, 1014b, 16 ff.
4 cf. particularly *Physics*, 193a, 1 ff.
5 cf. *Phys.*, 187a, 11 ff.
6 *Ibid.*, 188b, 37 ff.
7 *Loc. cit.*
8 Plato, *Meno*, 81d.
9 cf. K. Riezler, *op. cit.*, p. 8 ff., on the meaning of φύσις in the Presocratic Philosophy. Also W. Szilasi, *Die Beziehungen zwischen Philosophie und Naturwissenschaft:* p. 148. Also M. Heidegger, *Holzwege:* cf. p. 31 or p. 315. Heidegger understands the traditional meaning of φύσις as: 'Das aufgehende in sich verweilende Walten (An-wesen)'.
10 *Meta.*, 1015a, 13 ff.
11 *Ibid.*, 1041b, 30 ff.

ousiai, and, again in line with tradition, characterizes it as an *arche* [12].

It is here that he is particularly careful to emphasize that he means to use the word *physis* in its widest meaning. He speaks of *ousiai*, substances, which are substances because they are

> formed according to *physis* and by *physis* and therefore *ousia* [substantiality] would seem to be this *physis* [natureness] [13].

Those *ousiai* which are formed 'by *physis*' seem to be the *physei onta*, and those which are formed 'according to *physis* (*qua eidos*) [14] comprise also the *techne onta*.

Both *physei onta* and *techne onta* are *ousiai* because they are determined by substantiality *qua* natureness. We shall in the next chapter deal with the *physis ousia*. Here we only wish to emphasize that Aristotle's conception of the *physis einai* or *on* was, at least to the extent that he expressly treated of it, close to its traditional meaning. For, as mentioned before in the Ninth Book, he referred to it as that

> which neither comes nor ceases to be... [15].

explaining that it constitutes itself, *i.e.*, manifests itself in its truth, as the a-synthetic whole of a pregiven unity of momenta [16] to be grasped in *noesis* only.

It was to this meaning of the *physis einai* or *on* that Aristotle obviously referred when he asserted that the '*episteme* which contemplates being as being' (*on he on*) searches for

> a *physis* to which the ultimate causes and principles belong necessarily and per se [17].

The 'ultimate causes and principles' are seen as the momenta of a unity which the philosophers of the Lyceum were charged to eclucidate.

Such an elucidation of the momenta of the *physis* of being, these principles and ultimate causes, should be carried out universally. In a different context, Aristotle observed:

---

[12] *Loc. cit.*
[13] *Op. cit.* 1041b, 29.
[14] *Ibid.*, 1015a, 13.
[15] *Ibid.*, 1041b, 28.
[16] See p. 21 *supra.*
[17] *Meta.*, 1003a, 28.

> ...we only know all things insofar as they are one and the same in the sense that something universal is present [18].

'To know', therefore, means 'to find and express that which is valid throughout'. The force of language quite often drives man to use a noun when he tries to express the sum of that which is valid throughout. That is the reason why *on* and *einai* are frequently translated as 'Being'. This translation is quite legitimate so long as it is brought out that the Aristotelian *on* or *einai* is not a hypostatized Being.

Aristotle often uses the verbal form: to be *einai*, instead of the present participle being *on*, and he probably does so to emphasize that for him being means an occurrence [19], 'inherent' in a particular; that it is an immanent, determining principle [20]. He also goes to great length to demonstrate that being is not a *genus*. If being were a *genus* then the *species* would not 'be' because the determinations of a *genus* must not be used in defining a *species* [21].

There is a danger that we might easily go astray if we did not emphasize again at this point what the students of the Lyceum were aiming for. They were exhorted, first of all [22], to look at all the con-crete particulars and to contemplate what they 'truly were'. Driven by the Aristotelian hunger for concreteness, they tried to establish 'that something' in which all these particulars are the same [23] insofar as they 'are'. We must therefore bear in mind that while the Aristotelian student intended to elucidate the natureness of the concrete particulars around him, he was not asked to abstract from their undefinable richness, the wealth of shades, movements, tensions. For his task was to articulate an indwelling principle, an *arche*, leaving the particulars intact as they were. He did not look for a transcendental principle.

---

[18] *Ibid.*, 999a, 28.
[19] This expression is used by K. Riezler in *Man Mutable and Immutable* (p. 343).
[20] cf. the discussions, pp. 23 and 35.
[21] cf. *Meta.*, 998b, 20 ff.
[22] The student of the Lyceum should, as a *philosophos*, as distinct from a *physikos* also keep the substantiality of those substances before his eyes which are, as such, 'separate and immutable'. cf. *Meta.*, 1069a, 18; also 1025b, 1 ff, particularly 1026a, 10 ff. Yet he was to start from the *physis* of con-crete things and *see* 'in them' that which is separable from matter. cf. *Ibid.*, 1026a, 10 ff. and 1026a, 30 ff. cf. *infra* p. 63 ff.
[23] Or at least 'analogous'. cf. *Ibid.*, 1071a, 31, 1070b, 18, 1070b, 25.

But how could the Aristotelian philosopher in his activity of *aletheuein qua noesis* 'touch' the *physis* of any particular existing thing or man without 'abstracting' from its merely natural existence? Have we not ourselves insisted that the *noesis* (*qua aletheuein*) penetrates into a realm of its own, that both the activity and the subject-matter are on a different plane?

This difficulty will persist so long as we do not make it clear to ourselves that the *physis* which the philosopher touches *is*, independent of his faculty or his willingness to think. The contrary is a modern version of man as *subjectum*. If we hold to the fundamental Eleatic proposition that man is given a role only insofar as he is privileged to think (*noein*) and to make manifest (*aletheuein*) and thereby to assist in making all things self-transparent, we shall see things differently.

Things *are* so ordered that, while accessible to all sorts of common-sense 'natural' acting and knowing, they also have a *qua* structure which makes them accessible, as *noeta*, to philosophical *noesis* that contemplates them *qua* be-ings[24]. In seizing on their *qua* structure, the philosopher does not deny that they have other ways-to-be.

To maintain that there are two ways of acting and knowing, *i.e.*, the natural way and the philosophical way, can no longer be misunderstood. It is not a Platonic bifurcation of two realms nor is it a modern idealistic-subjective attitude. It is nothing but the reflection of the ways things and men 'are'. They are so structured that they are accessible in two ways. This seems to us to be the Aristotelian position. They may be accessible in more than two ways, but man may not, or not yet, have developed the faculty by which to reach them.

With these considerations in mind, we ask now: What is the character of this *noeton* that the philosopher un-conceals in this '*episteme* which contemplates being as being'?

We may deduce from our exposition of any *noeton* that 'being' as an asynthetic whole reveals itself, *i.e.*, constitutes itself in the noetic act as the unity of its pregiven momenta, and that this *asyntheton* is given beyond chronological time.

Furthermore, it has already been noted that Aristotle de-

---

[24] ὄν *qua* ὄν.

scribed 'being' as a *physis*, to which the *archai* and ultimate *aitiai* belong necessarily and per se. We know that 'being' is thereby characterized as a natureness, as the organizing principle and cause determining the ways the particular natures or 'beings' (*onta*) move.

In the Fifth Book, the book of definitions of the *Metaphysics*, Aristotle has also set out to define 'being' [25]. However, when dealing with 'being as such' [26], he actually does not explain it, but refers us to the *schemata of categories*, to the 'many ways one speaks about being' [27].

This is the formula which Aristotle repeats in many parts of his works [28]. The basic thought underlying it is the Eleatic assumption that man, 'the being that has *Logos*, speech (*zoon logon echon*), has been given the role of assisting in the unveiling of the *kosmos* [29]. The predicates of speech make the basic order of all-that-is manifest. That is why Aristotle says:

> The kinds of being as such are precisely indicated by the *schemata* of categories for the senses of being are just as many as these figures. Since, then, some predicates indicate what the subject is, others quantity, others quality or other relations, others activity or passivity, others its where, others its when, being has a meaning answering to these [30].

For Aristotle speech is carried on about something 'significant' [31]. It is a process by which 'meaning' is established. This occurs as man

> ...speaks about something as something [32].

Such a *legein kata tinos* is a *categorein*. Through joining, *synthesis*, and separating, *dihairesis*, the categorial predications are referred to a *subjectum* [33].

In the *Categories* these categorial determinations are described

---

[25] *Meta.*, 1017a, 8. καθ'αὑτὰ δέ εἶναι λέγεται.
[26] *Ibid.*, 1017a, 22.
[27] *Ibid.*, 1017a, 23. τὰ σχήματα τῆς κατηγορίας.
[28] cf. *Meta.*, 1028, 10, or *Phys.*, 185a, 30 ff.
[29] cf. p. 11 ff. *supra*.
[30] *Meta.*, 1017a, 23.
[31] *De Interpretatione*, 16b, 26.
[32] *Ibid.*, 17a, 24.
[33] See also p. 39 *infra*.

in more detail. Here they are expressly designated as *non-syntheta* [34].

Thus, while everyday speech makes use of these *asyntheta* in discursive thinking, and in this way 'collects' them into a unity, we know from our previous analysis that in philosophical *noesis* the unity of the *asyntheta* reveals itself in a different way. Here the *legein* would mean elucidating the momenta of the unity of this whole. We do not find, in the *Metaphysics*, that Aristotle tried to elucidate the inner meaning of the *asyntheton*, 'being as such', other than through an elucidation of the categorial ways in which it elucidates itself in speech.

The first sentence of the Second Chapter of Book Γ repeats this fundamental Aristotelian proposition that speech, in its categorial ways, elucidates the various meanings of being. But it does not go beyond this general insight. This is disappointing because the first passage held out the promise that it was now actually going to develop the *episteme* about 'being as such'. We had reason to hope that Aristotle would now explain the *noeton*, the *physis* of being, and articulate the modes of the asynthetic whole, to show in which way it is a natureness of natures.

Instead, we find ourselves reminded of the categorial ways 'being' elucidates itself in man's speech, and the rest as all of the *Metaphysics*, in fact, is an attempt to show how one of these categories is first (πρώτον) because all the other categories are related to it. Book Γ, 2, demonstrates this, and the way in which *ousia* determines all the other categories.

At the decisive point, therefore, Aristotle stops. Did he thereby want to tell us that man can really never know more about the meaning of 'being as such'; that all man may ever hope to grasp is the inner meaning of the categories, and particularly of *ousia*? Did he thus, anteceding Locke and Kant by 2000 years, want to set the borderlines up to which man might go, but never pass beyond? We do not know.

At any rate, through this strange way of holding out a promise in the first paragraph of Book Γ and disappointing his students in the second, Aristotle most forcefully expresses his conviction that the *episteme*, this philosophical *noesis* which contemplates,

---

[34] *Categories*, 1b, 25.

grasps, being as being, can never be more than an '*episteme* which contemplates *ousia*'. He might thereby have wanted to serve notice on us that his 'ontology' is in fact *not* a *logos tou ontos*, an explanation of the inner meaning of *on*, being, but is a *logos tes ousia*, an explanation of the inner meaning of *ousia*, substance.

We must emphasize that Aristotle clearly recognized that 'being' and one of the categories, substantiality, are not the same. He expressly stated that he wanted to treat the question, *what is being*? as if it were the same as the question, *what is substance*? [35]

> And, indeed, the question which was raised of old and is raised now and will always be raised and stirs us to amazement is the question what is being? and this is just the question what is substance?

We, who want to inquire into 'the meaning of Aristotle's ontology', have therefore no alternative but to acknowledge this fact and, following him, inquire into the 'meaning of *ousia*'.

[35] *Meta.*, 1028b, 3.

CHAPTER IV

THE *PHYSIS OUSIA*

The Second Chapter of Book Γ gives various illustrations to exemplify the way Aristotle wanted the students of the Lyceum to understand how the *legein* of all-that-is makes manifest that it 'is related to one certain *physis*'.

> Everything which is healthy is related to health; one thing in the sense that it preserves health, another in the sense that it produces it, another in the sense that it is a symptom of health, another because it is capable of it. And that which is medical is related to the medical art, one thing being called medical because it possesses it [this art], another because it is naturally adapted to it, another because it is a function of the medical art.

What is health? What is medical art? Health cannot be located in the color of the skin, nor can one find medical art embodied in the knife or in discussions or in this liquid called medicine. In fact, skin, knife, discussion, liquid have 'physical' properties, have structures which allow them to be defined as members of a class, as belonging to one 'common notion' [1]. There is a chemical formula for liquid medicine. This formula does not contain either health or medical art as an element. The knife is made of steel and wood. This definition of a knife does not tie it in any way to medical art.

Yet it is a fact that the color of the skin is indicative of health, that the medicine is 'conducive' to health, that the knife is useful for medical art, that the medicine is 'healthy' and so related to medical arts.

---

[1] cf. *Meta.*, 1003b, 13. τῶν καθ' ἓν λεγομένων.

Aristotle recognizes thus clearly that things are structured in two ways. We shall here, however, at present not deal with the ***kat' hen*** order of things which orders them in such a way that they can be classified by univocal definitions into classes of *genera* and *species*; however, cf. the definitional approach, p. 41 *infra*.

So, all these things have a 'second' structure, one which relates them to health or medical art, whereby health and medical art are 'that from which they get their meaning' [2]. They are the determinants determining that this skin 'means' a healthy skin, and this knife 'means' a medical knife.

Again, skin and knife are so ordered that they can receive such a meaning. This 'determining process' of giving and of receiving meaning must have occurred 'beyond time'; for prior to any natural encounter with the skin or the knife, the skin 'means' a healthy skin and the knife 'means' a medical knife. Health and medical art have pre-structured the skin and the knife.

Aristotle does not explain here how this determining or pre-structuring process takes place. There was really no need to, because these illustrations are only examples of eidetic determination and must therefore be understood in the same way as Aristotle understands the way that the *eide* pre-form the intelligible world [3].

We have now to apply the lesson which the illustrations exemplified to an understanding of the way in which-all-that-is is related to *ousia*.

We should note, first, that the word *ousia* is used in this context on the same level as health or medical art, and not on the level of 'healthy things' or 'medical things'. We established that health and medical art were determinants. It therefore follows from these illustrations that Aristotle used the term *ousia* here in the sense of a determinant. This is important to realize because Aristotle used the term *ousia* in many ways.

At times he even used the word *ousia* in the unphilosophical language in which also Homer used it, when he spoke of the *ousiai* of the fishermen, meaning their properties, their nets and boats. Or, again, Aristotle used the word ousia on the level of *episteme* as such, in calling the elements *ousiai* which should be investigated empirically.

Our concern is with the meaning of *ousia* for the 'philosophical attitude'. For we have satisfied ourselves that the passages which

---

[2] cf. *Ibid.*, 1003b, 18. δι' ὃ λέγονται.

[3] cf. p. 45 *infra*.

we are interpreting to find 'the meaning of ontology' are strictly meant for the philosopher.

Since it has been shown that Aristotle used the word *ousia* as a determinant, it might be preferable to translate it *substantiality*, as differentiated from *substance*.

Following the example set by the illustrations, Aristotle may thus have wanted to bring out that the various categorial ways-to-be are determined by substantiality. It is substantiality from which they 'depend and get their meaning...' [4], and they all can and must receive this meaning ultimately from this determinant. They are all 'related to (*pros hen*) a unity' [5], substantiality.

In philosophical *legein*, which is different from the *legein* of discursive thinking [6], the unity of this 'relatedness' is brought to light. Philosophical *noesis* grasps the substantiality of substances, an *asyntheton*, as expressly stated in the *Categories* [7] and in the *Metaphysics* [8]. Thereby the 'relatedness' is made explicit; for it is seen that the substantiality determines the substances-to-be *qua* substances, and that the substances receive their meaning from substantiality.

Just as the philosopher can 'see' that health has determined things to be healthy prior to the natural encounter, so the philosopher, in the noetic act, 'sees' that substantiality has already, or *a priori*, pre-structured the various ways-to-be of things and men as 'substantial' structures. The substantial structure, the substantial order, its *logos*, is 'given' beyond time, and discloses itself as such to human knowledge.

It is in this sense that the famous passage in Book [9] Z should be read:

> There are many ways one speaks about *proton* [first] but in any case *ousia* (substantiality] is a first with respect to *logos*, to *gnosis* and to *chronos* [chronological time].

This passage goes on to assert that all the ways-to-be of any particular, that is ,all its various categorial forms, cannot

---

[4] *Meta.*, 1003b, 18.
[5] *Ibid.*, 1003a, 33; 1003b, 14.
[6] cf. p. 17 *supra*.
[7] *Cat.*, 1b, 25.
[8] *Meta.*, 1075a, 5 ff.
[9] *Ibid.*, 1028a, 35.

'exist independently' [10]. They depend on substantiality because it determines all of them.

> It is that which is *proton* [first] and on which the other things depend and from which they get their meaning [11].

As Book Γ, 2, states, all these categorial ways-to-be make visible (through *legein*) a structure that 'relates them to one certain *physis*' [12].

We know that *physis* as a determinant means a natureness [13] and that the determining power is a natureness which is characterized as an *arche* or an *aition*. Here in Book Γ, 2, this one certain *physis* is expressly called an *arche* [14].

At the end of Book Γ, as we shall explain in detail later, this theme is taken up again. After naming *ousia* an *arche* and a cause [15], Aristotle states that

> all [particular] substances are constituted in accordance with and by a *physis* [16]....

and he concludes from this observation:

> *Ousia* would seem to be this *physis* which is not an element but an *arche* [17].

And *ousia* is here characterized as

> the first [*proton*] cause of being [einai)... [18].

of the particular *ousiai*.

We might therefore conclude that Aristotle clearly intended to grant to natureness, *ousia*, the rank and status which, in the first chapter, he gave to natureness, *on* or *einai*.

We thus find reaffirmed what Aristotle wanted to teach us: man contemplating 'being as being', trying to find the natureness, 'being as such', dicovers that only the natureness of substanti-

---

[10] *Ibid.*, 1028a, 36.
[11] *Ibid.*, 1003b, 17.
[12] *Ibid.*, 1003a, 33.
[13] cf. p. 23 *supra*.
[14] *Meta.*, 1003b, 7.
[15] *Ibid.*, 1041a, 10.
[16] *Ibid.*, 1041a, 30.
[17] *Ibid.*, 1041b, 30.
[18] *Ibid.*, 1041a, 10.

ality is accessible to him. Therefore, instead of looking for the 'ultimate causes and principles of being as such', he must confine himself to finding the principles and causes of substantiality.

> If then this is *ousia* (that which is primary and on which the other things depend and from which they get their meaning) it will be of *ousia* that the philosopher must grasp the principles and the causes [19].

[19] *Ibid.*, 1003b, 18.

CHAPTER V

OUSIA AND *OUSIAI*

The Second Chapter of Book Γ, as we have seen, demonstrates how *ousia* as substantiality determines the way men and things are *qua* substances, the way they 'substantiate'. All particulars are so structured that they can 'receive' such determination. They have a relational structure which relates them to this 'one certain *physis*'.

It would now be entirely un-Aristotelian and would constitute a radical misunderstanding to construe this *physis ousia* as a transcendental principle determining the particular *ousiai* 'from outside'. If one is to apply these modern categories at all, it must be maintained that the *physis ousia* is definitely an immanent principle. Substantiality 'dwells inside' every particular and thereby establishes it, founds it, grounds it, determines it, enables it 'to be' *qua* substance. It is a natureness and, as such, an *arche* [1].

Does this mean that there is, therefore, not a difference between substantiality (*ousia*) and particular substances (*ousiai*)? When we raise the question of a difference in this way, it is clear that we are not asking whether there is a difference between the way substances are related to (*pros hen*) substantiality, and the way things and men are ordered, *kat' hen*. We do not inquire into the difference between the 'two *logoi*', as K. Riezler [2] does.

We simply ask now: Is there a difference between the indwelling substantiality and the actual ways of things and men 'to substantiate'? Or, more important still: Does Aristotle indicate such a difference?

On first inspection, the text of Book Γ, 2, gives one the impression that Aristotle sees a difference. On the one hand:

---

[1] cf. p. 23 ff. *supra*.

[2] e.g. *Man, Mutable and Immutable*, 319 ff.

things and men have a relational structure that can receive 'meanings' from the certain one, *physis ousia*; and, on the other hand, there is this determinant *ousia* 'giving' such meaning in a relational way [3]. But if we keep in mind that this *physis* is an immanent principle, then it appears that this substantiality which dwells in every substance and thereby causes it to 'substantiate' is identical with all the ways-to-substantiate [4]. For to be a substance is nothing but the way of every particular 'to substantiate'.

The philosophical *noesis*, by recognizing in any particular the ways-to-substantiate, thereby touches its substantiality. 'Seeing' the ways-to-substantiate of a particular means just this: to recognize this or that mode as a pregiven moment of the unity of the a-synthetic whole, of this *noeton* called substantiality.

It therefore appears to be quite legitimate to translate this unity of modes by using the noun, substantiality, so long as one emphasizes that this substantiality is nothing but the whole of a unity of various modes by which a particular substantiates, and consequently 'is' *qua* substance.

The Aristotlian philosopher, we need to remind ourselves, certainly directs his eye to the many (*polla*) substances, the *ousiai*, because he does not dialectically discuss an idea abstracted from them. However, what he tries to see *in* them are the modes-to-substantiate; and these modes he sees as momenta of the one pregiven unity of substantiality. Therefore, it follows that substances 'have' substantiality only insofar as they 'are' *qua* substances. The substantiality elucidates the constitution of every particular. It is the *logos* of its 'blueprint', its ousiological structure which is to be elucidated insofar as it inheres in the particular.

The Book Γ, 2, lists various categorial ways-to-be of particulars. Of all of them Aristotle asserts that they are modes or ways-to-substantiate (and insofar as they substantiate they 'are'). Of course, just as the medical knife also answers to a classifying definition, namely steel plus wood, or the medicinal liquid can be described according to its chemical formula, so

---

[3] cf. p. 30 ff. *supra*.

[4] cf. *Meta.*, 1017b, 15 and 1028 a,35.

these ways of things and men can also be defined *kat' hen* without reference to substantiality.

One can attempt to order everything according to generic differences or according to similar 'projects' of classification. But these projects do not pay attention to the relational structure of things and men. It is the relational structure which philosophical thought follows and reveals when it sees that all these ways of things and men are related to a unity and to one certain *physis*. Every individual particular and its way is then un-concealed as a mode of substantiality. The structure is relational in the sense that this indwelling mode is only a mode insofar as it relates to the unity. It is not a 'part' of an agglomeration of parts, but as a mode is an ingredient of a whole; and the whole is always also 'present' where only one mode reveals itself.

Whether, and in what manner, this is possible should be shown in the same concrete way as Aristotle articulates the *logos* of *ousia*. This is achieved in the body of his *Metaphysics*. While it is not our task to explain Aristotle's entire Doctrine of Substantiality in all its facets, we have nevertheless to show, and thereby test our interpretation, what it means in concrete terms that the *noesis* of the philosopher possesses and sees the *noeton*, the *asyntheton*, the whole of the natureness substantiality as it constitutes itself, manifesting as a structured unity of pregiven momenta indwelling in particulars insofar as they 'are' *qua* substance.

CHAPTER VI

THE OUSIOLOGY

1. Method and Goal

Aristotle's treatment of *ousia* as he developed it in his *Metaphysics* does not present itself as a unified and thoroughly consistent body of thoughts. Therefore, to spell out the substantiality of substances in his work is something not altogether easy to accomplish.

Aristotle attacked his problem from many angles without showing in every instance how these various approaches refer to the same thing. It is therefore necessary for the interpretation to keep in sight that all his varying determinations of substantiality aim at an identical goal. This goal is to un-conceal, by bringing to speech and concept, the basic structure of all that is, in order to show that this basic core is one and the same[1] for and in every particular, and that it is given prior to any 'natural' encounter.

Why then did Aristotle treat of his subject-matter in such a disjointed way? The answer is: Aristotle did not develop the determinations of *ousia* as one interconnecting system of available 'tools' so that the philosopher might simply use them and thereby articulate the unity of substantiality as pregiven in any particular that he might encounter.

On the contrary, Aristotle's presentation must itself be understood as an un-concealing effort. It shows this philosopher, Aristotle, at work, and the ways he himself uses to un-cover. We observe him as he tries to reach his goal, once approaching from this aspect, then again from another. The *Metaphysics* are a true document of these labors. And the interpreter cannot do

[1] Or at least analogous. cf. *Meta.*, 1070a, 31, 1070b, 18, 1070b, 25 ff.

justice to this monumental work, if he does not keep clearly before his eyes what Aristotle himself understood ontology to mean. It is the interpreter's task to demonstrate how all these varying efforts were meant to explain substantiality. He has to show whether, and to what extent, they are either 'on the way' or have already reached the goal of demonstrating substantiality as the noetic whole of a unity of pregiven momenta, indwelling in a particular, and grasped prior to any natural encounter.

If one takes Aristotle's various versions of *ousia* in piecemeal fashion, most of them fall short of this goal. However, we have emphasized that they must be read together as they all strive to reach one and the same aim: to articulate the pregiven unity of substantiality.

We shall now attempt to demonstrate, and thereby try to justify our interpretation, that the *prote philosophia* is mainly an 'ousiology' revealing various approaches by which to articulate momenta of the noetic unity of the substantiality of substances.

2. *The Grammatical Approach, the Definitional Approach*

Aristotle directs his attention to the *tode ti* [2], to the 'this', the particular as it is encountered. Since he maintains that it 'is' *qua* substance, then he must show that this *tode ti* expresses its substantiality to the noetic 'seeing' of the philosopher.

Agristotle's first approach to this end is often called a 'grammatical' one because he emphasizes here that the *tode ti* is *ousia* insofar as it is *subjectum*. However, this *subjectum* is, on closer inspection, more than merely a grammatical subject of a sentence.

In the *Categories* Aristotle defines *ousia* as that which

> is neither asserted of a *subjectum* (*hypokeimenon*) nor is the *subjectum* [3].

and, according to Book Z of the *Metaphysics*,

> the *hypokeimenon* is that of which everything else is predicated while it is itself not predicated of anything [4].

---

[2] cf. *Meta.*, 1029a, 28, or 1028a, 12.
[3] *Cat.*, IIa, 11.
[4] *Meta.*, 1029a, 1; also 1017b, 14.

These statements are not only pronouncements about grammar. They contain a great deal of Aristotle's doctrine of *ousia*. He gives here a 'first name' to the *tode ti*. The philosopher 'sees' that basically every *tode ti* 'is' *qua ousia*. Its substantiality, the first category, lies, in a determining way, at the basis of all the other categories. Substantiality is, in this sense, the *hypokeimenon*. This is the same description of the determining power of the first category, of substantiality, which was earlier discussed in interpreting the Second Chapter of Book Γ; all the other categories are related to (*pros hen*) substantiality. Here it is repeated that they 'rest' on it.

The term *hypokeimenon* was translated as *subjectum*, indicating 'that which is thrown (*iacere*) under (*sub*) the other categories, but it was also translated as *substratum*. The latter translation led to many misinterpretations, particularly the one that 'matter' is the bearer of the *tode ti*. But Aristotle very explicitly rejected the view that, in this context, matter could be the *hypokeimenon*. He says that such a view 'is impossible' [5].

From the foregoing [6] it is, indeed, evident that Aristotle could not have meant that the determining power of the *tode ti* could be matter. For the *tode ti* is characterized as self-subsistent [7], as something definite [8], as an individual [9], and is equated with the what-a-thing-is [10]. On the other hand, matter is characterized as something entirely indeterminate. We shall deal with the meaning of Aristotelian 'matter' later on [11], and will here only quote his definition of matter in this particular context:

> By matter I mean that which is in itself neither a particular thing nor of a certain quantity not assigned to any other of the categories by which being is determined [12].

Obviously, something that is itself indeterminate in such a way could not have been meant by Aristotle to possess the

---

[5] *Ibid.*, 1029a, 28.
[6] *Ibid.*, 1028a, 10 ff.
[7] *Ibid.*, 1028a, 23.
[8] *Ibid.*, 1028a, 27.
[9] *Loc. cit.*
[10] *Op. cit.*, 1028a, 12.
[11] cf. p. 48 *infra*.
[12] *Meta.*, 1029a, 19 ff.

power to determine a *tode ti* as a determinate definite something.

Aristotle rather told us here that the *tode ti* is determined by substantiality and the substantiality has received the name *hypokeimenon*. This first name gives, in a negative way, certain indications about the meaning of substantiality [13].

By using this designation and definition: *subjectum*, Aristotle emphasizes that substantiality is definitely not that which 'is' only by virtue of the fact that is 'in' a *subjectum*. The other categories, such as qualities, like colors, 'are' only because they are 'in' a *subjectum*; the color white can not subsist as such. It owes the fact that it 'is' to the *sub-jecta* in which it happens to be; it is, therefore, only an 'accident'.

This negative statement leads to the positive result: if substantiality is not a mere accident 'in' others, then it follows that it is, in contradistinction, 'in' itself. And if substantiality is not 'for' others, then it follows that it is 'for' itself.

Second, if predicates and accidents subsist only because substantiality *qua subjectum* empowers them to subsist, then it follows that it is a power that can bestow subsistence. The positive result of the grammatical approach is, therefore, the identification of substantiality *qua hypokeimenon* as 'a power that is in itself and for itself and bestows subsistence on the other categories'.

It is now our task to demonstrate that Aristotle saw this self-subsisting power, determining a *tode ti*, as the whole of a unity of pregiven momenta, manifesting itself in the *noesis* of the philosopher prior to natural knowing and beyond chronological time. We next have to introduce additional approaches to articulate the meaning of *ousia*, namely, the definitional approach, the form-matter approach, the act-potency approach, and the causal approach.

But is this attempt not condemned to failure by Aristotle's own definition of *ousia qua hypokeimenon*? If *ousia* is only a 'bearer' of predicates, then this means that *ousia* itself can never be reached by a predicate. Indeed, as we shall show, Aristotle seems to have held that the very core of *ousia* can never be reached by the definitional approach; but it is a different

---

[13] cf. E. Gilson, *Being and Some Philosophers*, p. 43 ff.

question whether it can not be 'articulated' as a power. Yet even the definitional approach can carry the philosopher very close to the heart of *ousia*. It is his task to keep on elucidating [14] and defining [15] the subsisting power and to encircle it by ever better and better predicates.

This assignment given to the philosopher carries an important implication. If Aristotle thought that it was possible for definitions at least to elucidate substantiality (if only to a certain extent), then substantiality must basically be something 'structured' or ordered (*logos*), and these structures must in a sense exist prior to the attempt to bring them to word by means of definitions.

The subsisting, determining power of *tode ti*, of a particular would not have been declared to be even approachable by definitions if it were an unlimited [16] power. Aristotle must have conceived it as a power that is limited, structured, ordered [17], because it lends itself to elucidation by definitions. This particular agglomeration of paper, for example, reveals to the defining effort structures which make it definable either as a bundle of wrapping material or as a book, but never as a piece or iron.

Aristotle indicates, therefore, through the very fact that he suggests the possibility of the definitional approach, that substantiality is basically 'something ordered', and that is why he attempts in this definitional approach, in Book Z, to proceed logically [18], and tries to bring the *logos* [19] of a *tode ti* to its definition (*horismos*). The translators use the word 'formula' for *logos*, which correctly indicates that this 'something' has the ordered structure of a formula. Now this something which reveals a certain order and, therefore, might be defined, this substantiality receives a second name at the beginning of the definitional approach, and it must first be discussed in order to understand better what it is that the philosopher should try to elucidate in definitions.

---

[14] cf. *Meta.*, 1029b, 21 or 1030a, 7.
[15] cf. *Ibid.*, 1030a, 7.
[16] ἄπειρον. cf. *Philebos*, 16a.
[17] πέρας.
[18] *Meta.*, 1029b, 13.
[19] e.g. *Ibid.*, 1029b, 21; or 1030a, 8, etc.

The new name is *to ti en einai* [20], which the English language can only translate into the word 'essence', a term filled with scholastic meanings, while the German language can render it into the much more adequate word 'Wesen'. The literary translation from Greek would be: the-what-was-being.

There seems to be agreement among the commentators that the imperfect 'was' is meant to indicate timeless being. The *ti*, the 'what' of a *tode ti*, is that which it always was and will be: its eternally pregiven way-to-be. The 'what' of this particular, its substance which, as the first and determining category, is rightfully called its substantiality, is through this new name characterized as that which expresses fundamentally what a *tode ti* 'always was, and always will be'. The word *einai*, as was pointed out before [21], denotes with equal emphasis that this substantiality 'never comes nor ceases to be'. Aristotle, significantly enough, has to fall back on 'being', in order to characterise *ousia*.

The *Categories* [22], as well as the *Metaphysics* [23], explain that, and in which way, *ousia* denotes the *ti estin*, the 'what-is' of a particular, thereby expressing 'that which is primarily [24]'.

For only 'when we say *what* a thing is' do we not speak about accidental categories, such as quality or quantity, *i.e.*, whether something is 'white or hot or three cubits long', but point to that which determines all these accidents, *i.e.*, the substantiality of the substances, 'a man or a God' [25].

In the *Categories* we further hear that

> the most distinctive mark of substance appears to be that while remaining numerically one and the same, it is capable of admitting contrary qualities [26].

Substantiality, over and above its power to denote the 'what' of a particular, is here recognized to be a unifying force which keeps manifold momenta together.

---

[20] *Ibid.*, 1029b, 11.
[21] cf. p. 21 *supra*.
[22] cf. *Cat.*, 1b, 25 ff.
[23] cf. particularly *Meta.*, 1028a, 14.
[24] *Ibid.*, 1028a, 14.
[25] cf. *Ibid.*, 1028a, 15 ff.
[26] *Cat.*, 4a, 10.

The same thought is now brought out by this new name for substantiality: *to ti en einai*. The what (*ti-estin*) of a *tode ti* is established as that which it always was and always will be. Its manifold ways-to-be are held together in one regulating unity. It is this unity of the essence (*to ti en einai*), the unity of the *asyntheton*, the *noeton*, which the philosopher 'sees' in the noetic act.

> In general the thought of those things which one grasps in their *to ti en einai* [essence] through *noesis* is indivisible, and cannot be separated either in chronological time, or in space or according to its *logos* [27].

It is now important to stress that Aristotle in Book Z, in his definitional approach, does not try to grasp the *to ti en einai* through *noesis*. Here he does not proceed *pros hen*, but he proceeds *kat' hen* [28]. He tries to catch the heart of the unity, which as such is given him, by starting from the generic classification and there defining the *differentiae* of the *species*, splitting the *species* more and more until he arrives at *infima species*. While this is not a discursive-synthetic but an analytical procedure, it is yet not a noetic articulation of the unity of a *noeton*. This is clearly recognized by Aristotle when he states almost at the end of his labors:

> But when we come to the concrete thing (*synholon*) like this circle, *i.e.*, one of the individual circles, whether as an *aistheton* or as a *noeton* (by noetic circles I mean those of the mathematics and by aisthetic those of bronze or wood), of these there is no definition. We apprehend them by *noesis* or by *aisthesis* [29].

Yet, Aristotle attempts the definitional approach. He tries to find the definition of the *to ti en einai* of particulars, hoping thereby to elucidate

> the *logos* of something primary [30].

Following the specific rules he establishes for this definitional procedure [31], he elucidates the substantiality, the essence, of man, as that of a 'two-legged living being' [32].

---

[27] *Meta.*, 1016b, 1.
[28] cf. p. 30 *supra*.
[29] *Meta.*, 1036a, 1 ff.
[30] *Ibid.*, 1030a, 10.
[31] cf. *Ibid.*, 1035b, 5 ff.; also 1037b, 8 ff. and 1038a, 1 ff.
[32] *Ibid.*, 1037b, 10 ff.

However, Aristotle recognizes that this non-noetic approach suffers from many *aporiai* which mainly result from the tragedy of human language which can never really reach the 'this' because all the categories it uses are universals which denote only 'a such' [33]. It is possible to define concavity, but you can not define snubnose [34], and real noses come as snubnoses. Likewise, you can, in a sense, define man's soul if you only concentrate on his form, but your definition does not really reach the *synholon*, man [35]. For the philosopher must know that

> to reduce all things thus to form and eliminate matter is useless labor. For some things surely are particular form in a particular matter, or particular things in a particular state [36].

The definitional approach thus proves partly a failure. It is not a truly philosophical approach resulting from a noetic attitude.

The other approaches seem to promise better results, as Aristotle states in a different [37] context:

> Clearly then, if people proceed thus in their usual manner of definition and speech, they can not explain and solve the aporia. But, if, as we say, one is form and one is matter and one is actuality and the other potentiality, the question will no longer be thought an *aporia* [38].

3. The Eidos-Hyle Approach, the Eidos-Steresis Approach

Our previous discussions all presupposed that substantiality in its essential whatness (*to ti en einai*) has the power to make itself manifest, that it is 'intelligible' to the philosopher. This assumption implied that Νοῦς has enlightened both the 'structure of substantiality' in this given *tode ti*, as well as the philosopher who 'sees' it. And that means, as was earlier explained, that substantiality of *to ti en einai* 'grants sight', that it is eidos [39], form.

---

[33] cf. *Ibid.*, 1003a, 10, the 12th *aporia*.
[34] cf. *Ibid.*, 1035a, 1 ff., or 1036b, 30.
[35] cf. *Ibid.*, 1036b, 21 ff.; 1037a, 26 ff. See also p. 48.
[36] *Ibid.*, 1036b, 20 ff.
[37] See *Ibid.*, 1045a, 8 ff. for the aporia of the τί αἴτιον τοῦ ἕν εἶναι.
[38] *Ibid.*, 1045a, 20.
[39] cf. *supra*, p. 16 fn. ἰδεῖν, to see.

By *eidos* I mean the *to ti en einai* of each thing and its *ousia* [40].

Eidos is thus the 'third name' for *ousia,* and this name implies, as we shall show, *hyle*-matter, at least where the substantiality of movable sensible substances is involved.

Aristotle explained the meaning of *eidos* in the numerous discussions about art and the artist. The artist 'sees' [41], he pre-visions the *eidos* of that which he wants to make. He has a unity, namely the unity of the manifoldness of different *morphai* (size, color, etc.) before his 'eyes'. Prior to his *techne,* prior to all 'natural' knowing and acting, the form as an *a priori* unity is given in [42] his soul.

Things are made by art whose *eidos* is contained in the soul [43].

Here it is expressed very clearly: the unity of structure, its *to ti en einai,* becomes intelligible by virtue of 'that which grants sight'. This *eidos,* of the *to ti en einai,* is immutably given [44]. It 'is not generated' [45] and, therefore, is beyond time.

> To make the bronze round is not to make the round of the bronze but something else; to produce the *eidos* in another medium [46].

In the same sense Aristotle states:

> It is obvious then that that which is spoken of as *eidos* and *ousia* is not produced [47].

For, if one should want to manufacture *eidos,*

> ...the process of generation would continue to infinity [48].

And this is also true for things not made by art. That is why Aristotle does not recognize any generation of *species.* In the sequence of generations of man, the *eidos* of man does not 'come

---

[40] *Meta.,* 1032b, 1, 2.
[41] Such seeing is in a sense also *noesis.* cf. *Ibid.,* 1032b, 17.
[42] cf. *Ibid.,* 1016b, 12: 'we do not call anything a one unless it has the unity of an *eidos*'.
[43] *Ibid.,* 1032b, 1.
[44] As differentiated from the 'concrete thing which gets its name from it'; cf. *Ibid.,* 1033b, 17.
[45] *Ibid.,* 1033b, 5; also 1033b, 16.
[46] *Ibid.,* 1033a, 32 ff.; also 1069b, 35 ff.
[47] *Ibid.,* 1033b, 16.
[48] *Ibid.,* 1033b, 4; cf. also 1069b, 35 ff.

nor cease to be' [49]. Therefore, he repeats over and over again: '...man begets man' [50].

These passages confirm that the basic structure of every particular thing is given. It presents itself as *eidos* prior to all 'natural' knowing.

When we discussed the definitional approach, we demonstrated to what extent the basic structures of the *tode ti* are, in an *a priori* way, marked off from those of a different *tode ti*. *Eidos* makes intelligible that the basic structures of this or any paper, for instance, can never be those 'of a piece of iron'. *Eidos* thus differentiates the basic structures of this *tode ti* from those of another *tode ti*.

But more important still, *eidos unifies in an immanent way*. It acts as 'the *indwelling* form' [51]. *Eidos* makes a particular thing manifest as the 'same' thing. It does not make any difference whether Socrates is today uncultured and tomorrow cultured [52], whether he is walking or sitting, whether he is young or old. *Eidos* reveals him as the 'same' prior to all 'natural' understanding.

In fact, the entire definitional approach would have been impossible if the particular did not persist as the 'identical' *Eidos* guards this *a priori* identity by revealing that the predicative changes are basically only various modes-to-be of one unity. The intelligible light of *eidos* collects the diverging 'rays' and reflects them as 'one and the same.' *Eidos* reveals the man Socrates in his manifold divergencies as one soul in which all its changes are co-present as eidetic changes. It is in this sense that Aristotle said:

> ...sameness is clearly a kind of unity [53].

It is the unity of the modes that are made manifest as the 'same'. It is the '*logos* of primary *ousia*' [54], which we have already demonstrated as being the unity of a whole called *to ti en einai*.

Socrates' 'soul' presents itself, prior to all empirical analysis,

---

[49] In this context it is not important that it is 'numerically' one, but only that it is 'formally' one. cf. *Ibid.*, 1033b, 30.

[50] *Ibid.*, 1032a, 25.

[51] *Ibid.*, 1045b, 19; 1037a, 29.

[52] *Ibid.*, 1018a, 7.

[53] *Loc. cit.*

[54] *Op. cit.*, 1037a, 28.

as such a unity of a substantiality, intelligible as a context of interlocking momenta which, grown together, can never be divorced from one another. Socrates is the 'same' in the sense of such a contextual unity.

It is still in another sense that *eidos* forms a unity of a whole. It 'in-forms' *hyle*. *Hyle* is seen by Aristotle as one member of a pair of strictly correlative ontological determinates. It denotes, primarily, 'the dark' which the illumination, *eidos*, must already have overcome in order 'to be' as an intelligible unit. For '... matter is unknowable in itself' [55]. However, the philosopher knows that, and in which way, this unfathomable 'dark' *hyle* belongs to the knowable *eidos* [56], and in which way it is implied in this preconceived ontological unity of *eidos* and *hyle*.

The philosopher knows that *hyle* is a *hypokeimenon* 'relative to' *eidos*. Relative to this *eidos*, *i.e.*, this house, those bricks and wood are *hyle*. For the *eidos* 'house' could not come to be unless *hyle* entered. The philosopher knows that natural as well as technical things (the technical things, in fact, seem to have served as paradigms for the conception of the form-matter dichotomy) have two ontological determinants, the one *eidos* implying the other, *hyle*. Both together are 'conditions for the possibility' of a *tode ti*.

Yet, of this pair *eidos* is the more important partner. While everyday language recognizes the *synholon* of the two determinants and speaks of the 'wooden statue' [57], the philosopher knows that the statueness and not the woodenness of the *tode ti* is decisive. The *eidos* is that 'by virtue of which' [58] a thing is this and not something else. And this 'by virtue of which'

> ...in the primary sense is the *eidos* and in a secondary sense is the *hyle* of each thing [59].

The first philosopher, differentiated from the *physikos*, directs his attention to the 'empowering powers', the necessary conditions by virtue of which each thing 'is'. For his *noein*, *eidos*

---

[55] *Ibid.*, 1036a, 1, 9.
[56] cf. *Ibid.*, 1036a, 6; matter can be 'seen' in intuition.
[57] cf. *Ibid.*, 1033a, 18.
[58] *Ibid.*, 1022a, 15a.
[59] *Ibid.*, 1022a, 18ff.; also *De An.*, 412a, 8.

and *hyle*, as *archai* which are not generated [60], articulate the substantiality of this particular (*tode ti*) substance. He 'sees' it as a *synholon*, a concretum, grown together as *eidos* and *hyle*. Such 'seeing' must not be misunderstood. It is *noesis*, an intuitive apprehending, 'omitting matter' [61].

The philosopher in his *theoria* contemplates the many particular beings and contemplates in which ways they are 'the same'. He recognizes that they all 'are' *qua* substances. Their substantiality determines their ways-to-be. And, articulating the unity of the substantiality of this particular *tode ti* that he encounters, be it a man or a stone or a dog or a statue, he sees how the 'same *archai*', the same principles or determinants, are 'at work' in any one of these *synholoi*. He sees the substantiality, the regulating unity, the *to ti en einai*, knowing that, and in which way, *hyle* is implied in that which has 'granted him this noetic sight', this *eidos*.

There is a second way in which *eidos* permits the philosopher to 'see' a unity. The philosopher knows that every given *eidos* is nothing but the privation, the absence, the *steresis*, of its contrary *eidos*.

> Even contraries have in a sense the same *eidos*, for the *ousia* of a privation is the opposite *ousia*, *e.g.*, health is the substance of disease (for disease is the absence of health) [62].

In this sense we can say that a specific *eidos* 'comes from its privation' [63], as for instance:

> It is from an invalid rather than from a man that a thing comes to be produced [64].

The *eidos* of the invalid is here seen as the privative *eidos* which, in this sense, is the *hypokeimenon* [65] from which proceeds its *antikeimenon*, the *eidos*, health.

This *metabole*, this turnover of contraries, their coming (*genesis*) and going (*phtora*) can be 'seen' by the philosopher as

---

[60] cf. *Meta.*, 1034b, 13 and 1069b, 35, for the position that *hyle* is not generated either.

[61] cf. *Ibid.*, 1075a, 2.

[62] *Ibid.*, 1032b, 4; see also 1069b, 34.

[63] *Ibid.*, 1033a, 10 ff.

[64] *Ibid.*, 1033a, 11.

[65] cf. *Phys.*, 190b, 1.

the articulation of the unity of complementary-prestructured momenta. He sees the absent mode 'present' as an *eidos* in its *modus deficiens*.

4. *The Potency-Act Approach*

This pair of correlative modes spells the determining power of *ousia* most forcefully. It reveals the way in which the immanent process of determination takes place, how these two interlocking momenta of a whole exert movement. By means of this approach, Aristotle can, first of all, show how the apparent schism of *hyle* and *eidos* is bridged, and that *hyle* and *eidos* become one.

> *Hyle* exists potentially (δύναμις) because it may attain to its *eidos*; but when it is act (ἐνέργεια), it is in its *eidos* [66].

A piece of gold is capable of becoming a statue, although it is not yet a statue. Gold is *hyle* relative to the statue. But in a finished golden statue, gold in a sense 'is' the statue. Now gold is intelligible *eidos* and actuality; while it does not express that which enables a statue 'to subsist as a statue', gold nevertheless 'is'; it is as the golden in the statue [67]. So Aristotle demonstrates that in a 'kinetic way' *hyle and eidos* are 'one'.

> As has been said, the proximate *hyle* and the *morphe* are one and the same thing, the one potentially and the other actually. Therefore, it is like asking what in general is the case of a unity and of a thing's being one. For each thing is a unity and the potential and the actual are somehow one. [68].

But rather than try to show how *hyle* and *eidos* unite, *qua hyle* and *eidos*, one might identify them as the moving forces, as the principles revealing how the natureness substantiality ...is *arche*, 'causing the *metabolai* in something' [69]. Although Aristotle states expressly of actuality only that 'it is *ousia*' [70], it is evident that potentiality is *implied* in actuality.

In fact, he begins by defining potentiality, differentiating

---

[66] *Meta.*, 1050a, 15, 17.
[67] *Ibid.*, 1033a, 5, 20.
[68] *Ibid.*, 1045b, 19, 22.
[69] *Ibid.*, 1046a, 11.
[70] *Ibid.*, 1050b, 2.

potentiality with regard to movement, *i.e.*, 'power' [71], from potentiality in a wider sense, or 'capacity' [72]. As for potentiality *qua* power, he sets apart 'the power to act' from 'the power to be acted on' [73], and sees them as two aspects of a unity [74].

Actuality is explained as the actuality 'of' that power (to act and to be acted on) and of that capacity; it is in this sense that actuality is implied in potentiality and potentiality is implied in actuality. They are a unity, and the philosopher sees them always as the unity of two pregiven momenta, as a pair of correlative momenta fettered together to spell the power of substantiality.

Actuality, moreover, is defined by way of an analogy to potentiality...

> As that which is building is to that which is capable of building and the waking to the sleeping and that which is seeing to that which has its eyes shut but has sight... [75].

Aristotle concludes with the observation that is important for us:

> Let actuality be defined by one member of this *antithesis*, and the potential by the other [76].

This second definition of actuality and potentiality reveals them more clearly still as the 'two sides' of one unity; they together, implied in each other, make the power of substantiality manifest, articulating its 'dynamic' and 'energetic' modes and the efficacy of its intrinsic operation.

For the philosopher, *dynamis*, is always silently present in *energeia*, and *energeia* is absently present in *dynamis*. Such co-presence implies the Whither, *dynamis* in a Whence, *energeia*, and a Whence in a Whither, and so makes an 'inner' movement visible. In this con-crete the movement of *dynamis* and *energeia* is fused, and the substantiality comes to life. It spells the 'realness' of the real, a realness which mere 'predicates' cannot reach.

---

71 *Ibid.*, 1046a, 1 ff.
72 *Ibid.*, 1048a, 31 ff.
73 *Ibid.*, 1046a, 13 ff.
74 *Ibid.*, 1046a, 19.
75 *Ibid.*, 1048b, 1 ff.
76 *Ibid.*, 1048b, 4.

What the definitional approach, the logical elucidation of the *to ti en einai*, could not accomplish, has now been achieved. In the inner density of this movement where every actuality is a potentiality and every potentiality an actuality, the *noesis* of the philosopher 'sees' the realness of the real. He 'experiences this experience' [77], and thus grasps this un-concealedness (*aletheia*) ... of substantiality in an entirely unconceptual way. Here it comes out very clearly that the philosophical *noesis* is not a 'conceptual', *i.e.*, definitional, way of knowing, but is an 'intuitive gathering-in'.

This 'experience of the experience' will be particularly strong when the philosopher 'touches the whole' of the unity of man's soul.

Here he can, as we say today, through reflection really experience how the correlating modes of act and potency are forged together. And this experience provides him with a model for all the other *sub-jecta* of the *kosmos*.

The philosopher experiences, in his *theoria*, the substantiality of the soul as it presses forward from the *dynamis* of its unfulfilled powers and capacities to their *energeia* and their *entelecheia*, fulfillment. He sees how all the un-actualized powers are silently present and determine the actualized powers of the soul: how the actualized powers influence and determine the unrealized powers [78]. Together they are the 'whole' of the unity of man's soul.

The philosopher apprehends the movement of the substantiality of the soul in every one of its acts. He 'sees through' the loudest, the strongest, the most beautiful act and knows that it is silently filled with 'acting upon', with suffering, with destruction and decay. He understands intuitively that the 'not-yet' of all the unrealized hopes, all the patience and waiting of the soul's potential, have their ways of pre-determining today's decisions, feelings and passions. He knows that man's soul is in this sense 'eternally' on the way, 'is' in-between [79]; and it is only in this in-between, where the modes of actuality and

---

[77] 'erfaehrt die Erfahrung'.
[78] cf. K. Riezler, *Physics and Reality*, Ch. VII.
[79] Plato, *Parmenides* 130 E ff.

potentiality intermingle, that man can say that he has reached fulfillment (ἐντελέχεια).

The text of *De Anima* explains best how the philosopher, going through the various approaches, grasps the meaning of the substantiality of the soul as the unity of actuality and potentiality. The human soul is identified as a substantiality (*ousia*)[80].

When seen through the definitional approach the soul is

> the definitive *logos* of a *to ti en einai*[81].

But since it is the *to ti en einai* of a body[82], and this body is *hyle*[83], the definitional appraoch which cannot reach *hyle* gives way to the *eidos-hyle* approach. This approach shows that the soul is a substantiality in the sense of an *eidos*[84], of a *hyle* which is hyle 'relative to' this *eidos*. The *eidos* soul determines this *hyle* to be a '*natural*' body, *i.e.*, to move on its own[85] and to be 'organized'[86]. The substantiality of the soul, its natureness, takes this *hyle*, body, in hand like a tool, organizes it, and thereby gives it its regulating unity.

As the *eidos-hyle* approach turns into the actuality-potentiality approach, the philosopher 'sees' how the unifying force of the substantiality of the soul operates. This approach shows that the potentiality is the 'power of life'[87].

The term 'life' (τὸ ζῆν)[88] embraces all the powers of the soul from the 'vegetative' to that highest power, in the case of man, which is really not a power or a potentiality any more[89], but an actuality[90].

The power of life uses an 'organ', called body. But this power (and its organ) is disclosed as only one side of a unity, the other side of which is the soul. The soul 'is' the first *entelecheia*, the

---

80 *De An.*, 412a, 11.
81 *Ibid.*, 412b, 12.
82 *Ibid.*, 412b, 13.
83 *Ibid.*, 421a, 17.
84 *Ibid.*, 412a, 20.
85 *Ibid.*, 415b, 23.
86 *De An.*, 412b, 1; also 421b, 5.
87 *Meta.*, 1015a, 13.
88 cf. *De An.*, 413b, 1, particularly 413 b, 10.
89 cf. *Ibid.*, 413b, 24; 415a, 12; *Meta.*, 1072b, 26.
90 cf. *De An.*, 430a, 23 ff.

fulfillment [91] of this power of life. Soul is thus clearly shown not to be a 'separate part' over against another 'separate part' called body, nor as a quality or a quantity but it is 'seen'; as a unity, and as Aristotle emphatically states at this point and within this context:

> Unity has many senses but the most proper and fundamental sense of both is the relation of an actuality to that which is the actuality [92].

The philosopher can see this unity of substantiality through still another approach: the causal [93], which needs to be considered next.

5. The Causal Approach

Aristotle tries to show through the causal approach how the *tode ti*, this composite sensible thing, reveals its substantiality as a natureness. An earlier chapter discussed the sense in which Aristotle identified substantiality with natureness, so that natureness is

> a kind of *arche* [principle] and *aition* [cause].

Cause is the fourth name that Aristotle gives to the substantiality of substances. This name is only a restatement of the other three names; the causal approach, however, makes the operative force of substantiality more visible. By asking the question: *dia ti*, the determinants that are 'responsible for' this *tode ti*, for its existence (*genesis*), and for its change (*metabole*), become manifest.

> Men do not think they know a thing till they have grasped the why of it (which is to grasp its primary cause [94]).

The causes in which the *tode ti* is grounded become explicit and reveal themselves as determining powers.

Except for the efficient cause, which is only an *arche*, the beginning of a movement [95], and which mostly acts from outside [96], (leaving the *tode ti* to its fate), the other causes – material

---

[91] *Ibid.*, 412a, 28. πρώτη ἐντελέχεια.
[92] *Ibid.*, 412b, 8.
[93] cf. *Ibid.*, 415b, 9 ff.
[94] *Phys.*, 194b, 20.
[95] *Meta.*, 1013a, 30.
[96] *Ibid.*, 1013a, 30.

cause, formal cause, final cause – 'stay with' the *tode ti* as determining powers and act immanently. They thus articulate the determining power of the substantiality of substances, 'moving' the *tode ti* from within. Here the full meaning of substantiality, as it has been developed throughout this discussion, comes fully to light.

The *cause* of this house or this man, of every house or man, is that there is 'such a thing' as house or man, something that makes possible the sight of a house or man: the *eidos* house and the *eidos* man. Their form is their cause.

The existence of a thing or a man, their thatness is not a problem to Aristotle, 'since we have the existence of something given' [97]; but the 'why' of the thing or of man is the question which stirs the philosopher to amazement. And this is not the 'why' of everyday questions, which asks most of the time for the 'efficient causes' of change. It is a 'why' that wants to unconceal what empowered this particular, this *tode ti*, to be this *tode ti*. It is such a question as: *why are these materials a house?* [98] or: *why is this individual thing, or this* body having this form, a man? [99]

What these questions seek to ascertain is:

> the *aitia*, the *eidos*, by virtue of which the matter is some definite thing... [100].

and, Aristotle continues,

> This is the substantiality of each thing [101].

The search for the formal cause is thus clearly recognized as the search for the substantiality of each thing. It poses the question aimed at bringing to light and articulating the unity of the determining, empowering, power which makes it possible at all that this substance 'is' *qua* substance. Aristotle knows that this is a problem for which not everyone has an ear. Most people will not even understand what the philosopher is talking about, for these 'simple terms' [102], these *a-syntheta* (the substantialities), are taken for granted.

---

[97] *Ibid.*, 1041b, 3.
[98] *Ibid.*, 1041b, 5.
[99] *Ibid.*, 1041b, 6, 7.
[100] *Ibid.*, 1041b, 5.
[101] *Loc. cit.*; cf. also 1043a, 2.
[102] *Op. cit.* 1041b, 10.

> Evidently, then, in the case of simple terms no inquiry nor teaching is possible; our attitude towards such things is other than that of inquiry [103].

It is only in the philosophical attitude that one can talk about substantiality. Substantiality is only accessible as a *noeton*. This has been our thesis all along, and we see it here confirmed.

Aristotle proceeds by presenting several examples to make it clear how substantiality *quà* natureness and formal cause empowers, determines, *a tode ti* to be *qua* substance.

> Since that which is compounded out of something in such a fashion *that the whole is one* (*hen*), not like a heap the way a syllable is, so the syllable is not its elements, *ba* is not the same as *b* and *a*, nor is flesh the same as fire and earth. For when these [elements] are separated, the wholes, *i.e.*, the syllable and the flesh, no longer exist, while the elements of the syllable still exist as do fire and earth; the syllable then is *something*, not only the elements (the vowel and the consonant) *but also something else*, and the flesh is not only fire and earth or the hot and the cold, but also *something else* [104].

The problem thus becomes, what is this 'something else' or 'other' by virtue of which *ba* is not just the letters *b*and *a*, but as this *tode ti* 'is' the substance called syllable; or by virtue of which the fire and earth in flesh are not just the elements fire and earth, but one substance called flesh. Aristotle answers:

> But it would seem that this 'other is something, and not an element and that it is the cause which makes this thing flesh and that a syllàble [105].

And he continues:

> and this is the substantiality of each thing for this is the primary cause of its being (*aition proton tou einai*) [106].

And this substantiality

> would seem to be a kind of natureness which is an *arche* [107].

---

[103] *Loc. cit.*
[104] *Op. cit.*, 1041b, 12 ff. (Author's italics).
[105] *Ibid.*, 1041b, 25 ff.
[106] *Ibid.*, 1041b, 26 ff.
[107] *Ibid.*, 1041b, 30.

We thus come a full circle: it was asserted and proved, at the beginning of the discussion, that the *episteme* which contemplates 'being as being' is a *noesis* which un-conceals the fact that particulars 'are' *qua* substances, inasmuch as they are determined by a natureness, an *arche* (and *aition*) substantiality. Here, in the body of Aristotle's ousiology, we find that the philosopher 'sees' how, prior to all 'natural' knowing in chronological time, this *arche* (and *aition*), this natureness substantiality, enables this *tode ti* 'to be' *qua* substance. Its *eidos* as the 'something else' has preformed, ordered, unified its elements in such a way that they present themselves as this particular substance.

The unfolding of the 'final cause' in conjunction with that of the 'material cause' reveals best in which way the determining power of substantiality exercises its determining force; and it is here that the various approaches of Aristotle's 'ousiology' coalesce and attain their climax.

The *eidos* fully perfected, the final form, makes manifest why – or 'for the good (*agathon*) of which' – this *tode ti* becomes, or 'is'. The philosopher who can 'see' the final goal, the *telos*, and in which way it acts, experiences the power of the substantiality of a substance and, thereby, apprehends the 'direction' of its operation.

A *telos* itself is unmoved [108]. However, it originates movement. The motive in man's mind, for example, his desire is itself unmoved; but it is an *aition* for the 'beginning of a movement' towards the fulfillment of this desire. The *telos* (final cause) thus 'causes' an *arche*; the *arche*, on the other hand, would not act as an *arche* were it not for the *telos*. The 'end' is in this sense the 'beginning' and the 'beginning' is the end [109].

It appears that the philosopher 'sees' the substantiality most effectively when he sees it operating as the 'final cause'. He then sees how this 'one certain *physis*' 'actually determines' the *tode ti* to be *qua* substance; how its *eidos* moves it so that it may 'come to its end', its *entelecheia*.

---

[108] *Phys.*, 198 b, 1.

[109] cf. G. W. Hegel: *Vorrede zur Phaenomenologie*: para. 18: 'Es ist das Werden seiner selbst, der Kreis, der sein Ende als seinen Zweck voraussetzt und zum Anfang hat und nur durch die Ausfuehrung und sein Ende wirklich ist'.

The philosopher who follows the way the determining power of substantiality as a final cause 'causes' the *tode ti* to become, to change, and to 'be', can see how this teleological directedness determines it at every step; he can see how the 'next step' acts as the *telos* for the 'preceding one'; how one serves the other [110] until the thing has arrived at its *telos*, and is essentially perfected: *teleion*.

We have already seen that in the case of man-made things, the *eidos* of the thing which should be perfected and, therefore, its final *eidos*, is already 'in the soul' of the technician [111]. Now the *techne*, *i.e.*, the *techne* to make a statue, of which this man, this *Technites* disposes, is that 'from whence the movement begins'; it is the 'efficient cause' of the statue.

> There are causes of the statue *qua* statue, one being the cause in which the motion begins [112].

But the *techne*, the skill to make a statue, is only an efficient cause of this statue, if the *technites*, the sculptor, has seen the fully perfected, final *eidos* (final cause) of the sculpture in his soul. Therefore, Aristotle says in the *Metaphysics*:

> ...for the medical *techne* and the building *techne* [read also sculpturing *techne*] are the *eidos* of the health or the house [or the sculpture] [113].

This *eidos*, as a *noeton*, is now seen as that for the 'sake of which' (*heneka tou*) the *techne*, the beginning of the movement, takes place. It is in this sense that Aristotle says:

> Therefore it follows that in a sense health comes from health and house from house [and sculpture from sculpture] [114].

In this way Aristotle made it clear that in the case of the *genesis* of technical things, *telos*, *eidos* and *arche* of movement are the same, or, in our terminology, that the substantiality of a thing (*i.e.*, a piece of sculpture) prestructures it, determines it from its inception and guides it to its perfection.

Aristotle explains [115] in which way the 'seeing'' (*noesis*) of the

---

110 *Phys.*, 194 b, 35 ff.
111 cf. *Ibid.*, 1032a, 34.
112 *Phys.*, 195a, 8.
113 *Meta.*, 1032b, 13.
114 *Loc. cit.*
115 *Op. cit.*, 1032b, 5 ff.; also particularly 1032b, 15 ff.

substantiality in technical processes determines the making (*poiesis*) of the sculpture. Through this analysis he shows how *hyle* as 'material cause', which is 'responsible' for the statue [116], is likewise determined by its substantiality. Or, as Aristotle says:

> That with matter comes from that without matter [117].

For, just as the substantiality *qua telos* house was shown to determine the *techne* of the technician, so that 'in a sense house comes from house', so the substantiality of the house determines what 'kind of' *hyle* is necessary to finalize the house.

The sculptor guided by the substantiality of this particular sculpture 'sees' that he needs this sort of material, gold, and this sort of material, wood, as the base, and so forth; or the architect knows that he needs these stones, that wood, these nails; their status as matter is thus determined by the sight of form, the final form, the substantiality of this particular house:

> For the helmsman knows and prescribes what sort of form a helm should have [118].

> For instance, why is a saw such as it is: to effect so and so and for the sake of so and so. This end, however, cannot be reached unless the saw is made of iron. It is therefore necessary for it to be of iron if we are to have a saw and perform the operation of sawing [119].

Aristotle explained the determining force of substantiality principally with reference to substantiality of technical things because, as has been mentioned before, his entire ousiology is oriented at *techne.*

> If a house had been a thing made by nature, it would have been made in the same way as it is now by art; and if the things made by nature were made also by art, they would come to be in the same way as by nature [120].

Yet, his wider concept of natureness, while in its widest sense also applicable to man-made things [121], shows in a particu-

---

[116] cf. *Phys.*, 195a, 5.
[117] *Meta.*, 1032b, 12.
[118] *Phys.*, 194b, ff.
[119] *Ibid.*, 200a, 11 ff.
[120] *Phys.*, 197a, 13 ff.
[121] cf. p. 24 *supra*.

larly clear way that the substantiality of natures is 'for the sake of something' [122]. The entire natural production occurs *heneka tou telos*.

> Our teeth should come up of necessity, the front teeth sharp fitted for tearing, the molars broad and useful for grinding down food [123].

Although there is no 'intelligent action' in nature of the kind we know as *techne* in man, it still appears

> that by natureness and for a *telos* the swallow makes its nest and the spider its web, and plants grow leaves for the sake of the fruit and send their roots down (not up) for the sake of nourishment [124].

And this appears to be so because these substances are not indifferent to each other, but are structured in such a way that they serve each other in order to reach a final goal. The natureness of nature, unless there is some impediment [125] or a 'mistake' [126], has structured them so that one substance serves the other.

> The preceding step is for the sake of the completion of the other [127].

The philosopher 'sees' this unity of *physis*. He grasps the many steps, the *metabolai*, as 'one' for he knows that natureness *qua telos* holds the 'beginning and the end' of all these steps together (*syneches*). He sees in the 'not-yet' of the seed the 'already' of the fruit; and in the already of the fruit he sees the not-yet of the seed. He knows that the substantiality, the form, the *telos*, are immutably given (causing the beginning of a movement that ultimately all leads back to this beginning). So just as Aristotle observed with respect to things made by *techne*, he says with reference to things made by nature:

> The beginning and the end fall together [128].

So here, in the same way as was the case with technical

[122] cf. *Phys.*, 198b, 10.
[123] *Ibid.*, 198b, 23.
[124] *Ibid.*, 199a, 27 ff.
[125] *Ibid.*, 199b, 25.
[126] *Ibid.*, 199a, 35 ff.
[127] *Ibid.*, 199a, 9.
[128] *De An.*, 423b, 23.

things, the natureness, the substantiality of the natural thing determines the *hyle* which is necessary to fulfill this substantial form [129].

Or, as Aristotle says in *De Anima*, with reference to the soul:

> It is manifest that the soul is also the final cause of the body. For nature, like Νοῦς, always does whatever it does for the sake of something which sometimes is its end [130].

In this final cause approach, the unity of soul and body, which the actuality-potentiality approach had already made manifest, reveals itself more clearly still. It can now be seen *why* '... all natural bodies are organs of the soul' [131], and that 'for the sake of which they are is soul' [132]. For the soul is both 'the end to achieve' [133], as well as 'the being in whose interest anything is done'' [134].

The philosopher sees ,for example, that natureness has provided a *hyle* called body, has 'organized' it so that the power of life can make use of it; and that thereby natureness, in this case the substantiality of the soul as the regulating unity, the *to ti en einai*, arrives at its fulfillment (*entelecheia*).

> For in everything the *to ti en einai* is identical with the *aition* of its being, and here in the case of living things, their being is to live, and of their being and their living, the soul is the cause and *arche* [135].

In sum, it is thus possible to see how, in the Aristotelian 'final cause', all his various other noetic articulations of substantiality coalesce; that, in a sense, they are all the 'same'. Preceding chapters have demonstrated:

1. that, and in which sense, the *to ti en einai* is the 'same' as the *eidos*.
2. that the *eidos* is the 'same' as *telos* and that the 'final' cause is, therefore, the 'same' as the 'formal' cause.
3. that the final cause 'causes' the 'beginning of the movement' and is, therefore, the 'same' as the efficient cause.

---

129 *Phys.*, 198a, 25.
130 *De An.*, 415b, 15 ff.
131 *Ibid.*, 415b, 18.
132 *Loc. cit.*
133 *Ibid.*
134 *Ibid.*
135 *Op. cit.*, 415b, 12 ff.

4. that *hyle* becomes *eidos*, and that their 'unity' manifests particularly clearly when they are seen as co-present in the modes of potency and actuality. In the 'final cause' approach, furthermore, it becomes manifest how the merely potential (*hyle*) is 'for the sake of' and is in this sense 'one' with its *eidos qua telos*.

Aristotle, it will be recalled, defined the task of the philosopher in the first book of *Metaphysics* as the 'search for the principles and the ultimate causes' [136]. In Book Γ [137] he specified this task more fully in saying that it was to 'look for the principles and ultimate causes of substantiality', and we have observed how Aristotle himself in his ousiology tried to do just that. As we have sought to show, this philosophic task demands a specific human attitude, the attitude of *noesis* which, as the *Nicomachean Ethics* makes clear, is that kind of *praxis* which fulfills (*entelecheia*) the human task (*ergon anthropinon*).

This search for the 'ultimate causes and principles of substantiality' is concentrated in the search for the 'final causes' only, since all other causes, as well as all other approaches translated into causal approaches, merge in this one. In due course the 'final causes' of natural and man-made things reveal themselves as the natureness of substantiality of the substance. Since substantiality, as the first category determining all the various categorial meanings of being, is the only humanly accessible expression of 'being as such', so the '*episteme* that contemplates being as being' is revealed finally as the *episteme* that contemplates *substantiality qua telos*, final cause.

The 'meaning' of Aristotle's 'ontology' is therefore an 'ousiology', and this ousiology is the *noesis* that 'sees' final causes which, themselves unmoved, move the universe of nature and *techne*.

But did Aristotle not also tell men that Philosophy is a 'divine science'? Did he not insist that in the noetic act, when man reaches his fulfillment, he is 'more than man', and in a sense 'divine' (θεῖόν)? [138] Did he not further tell us that ὁ θεὸς

[136] *Meta.*, 981b, 25 ff.
[137] *Ibid.*, 1003b, 18.
[138] *Nic. Eth.*, 1177a, 10 ff. cf. p. 12 *infra*.

is among the 'causes' of all things and is a principle ,*arche*? [139]

Aristotle hints in the *Theology* at the substantiality [140] of ὁ θεὸς. His explanations are not of the substantiality of a 'concrete being', although he uses the word *zoon* (ζῷον). For ὁ θεὸς is not a *tode ti*, a particular that needs a *metabole*, one whose *eidos* would, therefore, only be intelligible by reference to *hyle* and whose actuality would imply potentiality. Rather, 'his' substantiality, if it can be grasped at all, can only be articulated as 'pure *eidos*' and 'pure *energeia*', making 'intelligible' the actuality of Νοῦς, the *Light* [141].

Elucidated through a causal approach the substantiality of ὁ θεὸς is 'final cause' [142]. Like every other 'final cause' ὁ θεὸς is unmoved [143], but originates the beginning of a movement [144]. 'He' is the 'beginning and the end' for the heavens and the *physis* [145].

Does Aristotle, by describing ὁ θεὸς as the 'final cause' [146], indicate that the *philo-sophos* should, when searching for the *tele* of natural and man-made things, at the same time search for this 'highest' *telos*?

We do not know. There is a great deal of merit in the view that the motifs of the *Theology* are unrelated to those of the other books of the *Metaphysics* [147]. However, leaving aside all arguments that are based on references to the *Theology* contained in the other books, particularly the Sixth Book, we are inclined to assert that the Aristotelian *philo-sophos* is basically and throughout the *Metaphysics* a *God*-lover and a *God*-seeker, insofar as the Aristotelian θεὸς is 'God'.

True, the philosopher directs his attention to the immense variety of con-crete beings around him. He wants to 'see' their substantiality and to 'contemplate' in which way their

---

139 *Meta.*, 983a, 8 ff.
140 *Ibid.*, 1072b, 25 ff. 1073a, 2 ff.
141 *Ibid.*, 1074b, 35.
142 *Ibid.*, 1072b, 1 ff.
143 *Ibid.*, 1072b, 8.
144 *Ibid.*, 1072b, 4.
145 *Ibid.*, 1072b, 13.
146 *Ibid.*, 1072b, 4.
147 Regarding this controversy cf. E. Zeller, *Aristotle and the Earlier Peripathetics*, I, p. 291; or W. Jaeger, *Aristotle*, p. 218; or W. D. Ross, *Aristotle's Metaphysics*, I, p. 252 ff.

tele are the 'same'. But the *philos-sophos* realizes that he can 'see' their substantiality only as a *noeton*, apprehended in a philosophical attitude, *noesis*. He knows, therefore, that Νοῦς must have enlightened him so that he can 'see', and that he could never grasp 'the first principles' without Νοῦς, nor would his *episteme* be *sophia* had not Νοῦς joined it [148]. It is in this awareness that a philosopher 'possesses' the substantiality of substances, the *eidos* 'in their images', knowing that these *eide* again, owe to Νοῦς their power 'to grant sight'.

Must this *philo-sophos* not forever, even when concentrating his attention on the *tele* of natural and man-made things, have the vision of Νοῦς before his eyes as the 'most beautiful' and the 'highest' and the 'perfect *eudaimonia*'? [149]

Is it really an 'unrelated motif', when Aristotle calls this 'pure actuality of Νοῦς', this νόησις νοήσεως, the actuality of ὁ θεὸς? [150] Or when he, who as a *philo-sophos* is prone to amazement, is 'compelled to wonder most' [151] about the substantiality' [152] of that pure actuality of *Nous*, and is thereby 'moved' to search for it lovingly'? [153]

One may ask whether it might not be said that the Aristotelian *philo-sophos* is both a servant and a lover of Νοῦς, and that Νοῦς is both the master and loved one. The seeker serves and loves Νοῦς in a twofold way, and in a twofold way Νοῦς reigns over him: he serves and loves Νοῦς 'in' his *sophia*, while Νοῦς 'in' *sophia* moves him to search passionately; and he serves and loves Νοῦς in its highest actuality as ὁ θεὸς, 'who' moves him to 'see' and to search for 'him' as the 'beginning and the end'.

Living a life devoted to Νοῦς, acting out the ἔργον ἀνθρώπινον, the 'human task', the philosopher tries to 'see' the 'cause and the causes', and it is in this way that he fulfills *the meaning of Aristotle's 'ontology'*.

---

[148] cf. p. 11 supra.
[149] *Meta.*, 1072a, 30 ff.
[150] *Ibid.*, 1072b, 20; 1072b, 27; 1074b, 35.
[151] *Ibid.*, 1072b, 24.
[152] *Ibid.*, 1073a, 2.
[153] *Ibid.*, 1072b, 4.

A SHORT BIBLIOGRAPHY

BROECKER, WALTER, *Aristoteles*, Klostermann, Frankfurt, 1935.

DIELS, HERMANN, *Die Fragmente der Vorsokratiker*, Weidmannsche Buchhandlung, Berlin, 1912.

GADAMER, HANS GEORG, *Zur Vorgeschichte der Metaphysik*, in 'Anteile', Klostermann, Frankfurt 1950.

GILSON, ETIENNE, *Being and some Philosophers*, Pontifical Institute, Toronto, 1949.

HARTMANN, NICOLAI, *Zur Grundlegung der Ontologie*, Anton Hain, Meisenheim, 1948.

HEGEL, G. W., *Phaenomenologie des Geistes*, Felix Meiner, Leipzig, 1949.

HEIDEGGER, MARTIN, *Sein und Zeit*, Max Niemeyer, Halle, 1949.
—— *Holzwege*, Klostermann, Frankfurt, 1950.
—— *'Logos' in Festschrift fuer Jantzen*, Mann, Berlin, 1952.

HUSSERL, EDMUND, *Ideen zu einer reinen Phaenomenologie und Phaenomenologischen Philosophie*, Bd. I, M. Nijhoff, Haag, 1952.

JAEGER, WERNER WILHELM, *Aristotle: Fundamentals of the History of his Development*. trans. Richard Robinson, Oxford, Clarendon Press, 1934; 2nd ed: 1948.

KANT, IMMANUEL, *Kritik der reinen Vernunft*, Felix Meiner, Leipzig, 1944.

OWENS, JOSEPH, *The Doctrine of Being in the Aristotelian Metaphysics*, Pontifical Institute, Toronto, 1951.

RIEZLER, KURT, *Parmenides*, Klostermann, Frankfurt, 1934.
—— *Physics and Reality*, Yale University Press, 1940.
—— *Man, Mutable and Immutable*, Regnery, Chicago, 1950.

ROSS, W. D., *Metaphysics, Introduction and Commentary* Vol. I and II, Oxford, Clarendon Press, 1st Edition, 1924.

SZILASI, WILHELM, *Macht und Ohnmacht des Geistes*, A. Francke A.G., 1946.
—— *Die Beziehungen zwischen Philosophie und Naturwissenschaft*, in 'Die Einheit unseres Wirklichkeitsbildes', Lehnen Verlag, München, 1952.
—— *Wissenschaft als Philosophie*, Europa Verlag, Zürich, 1945.

WEISS, HELENE, *Kausalitaet und Zufall in der Philosophie des Aristoteles*, Haus zum Falken, Basel 1942.

ZELLER, EDUARD, *Aristotle and the Earlier Peripathetics*. trans. B.F.C. Costelloe and J. R. Muirhead, Longmans, Green and Co., London, New York, etc. 1897.

INDEX

Made in the USA
Las Vegas, NV
14 November 2024

11640401R00046